SCHOOLING
WITH
GROUND POLES

CLAIRE LILLEY

SCHOOLING WITH GROUND POLES

Flatwork Schooling for Every Horse and Rider

J. A. ALLEN

This book is dedicated

to

My Dad

© Claire Lilley 2003
First published in Great Britain 2003

ISBN 0 85131 864 9

J.A. Allen
Clerkenwell House
Clerkenwell Green
London EC1R 0HT

J.A. Allen is an imprint of Robert Hale Limited

A catalogue record for this book is available from the British Library

Design by Judy Linard
Edited by Jane Lake
Illustrated by Claire Lilley, Jean Hansen and Maggie Raynor
Colour separation by Tenon & Polert Colour Scanning Limited, Hong Kong
Printed by Midas Printing International Limited, China

Contents

Acknowledgements

There are many people to whom I owe a debt of gratitude for encouraging me and giving me the confidence to write this book but too many to name individually. Thank you all.

I am very grateful to the riding stables and equestrian centres that allowed me to use their facilities, namely West Lavington Equestrian Centre, Wiltshire, Allmanor Park Livery Stables in Surrey, Ulla and Steve Haygood at Nobynas Friesian Stud in Sweden and Liz and Richard Stevens of www.horsedata.co.uk

Also, many thanks to the riders and horses who have appeared in the book: Anna Backman-Klein and Turbo, Lena Hutterstrom and Furiosa, Sue Watson and Demi, Rhonda Belchamber and Fabuloso, Matthew Cox and All the Rage, and Emma Ballardie and Mickey. My own horse, Carina Amadeus, also deserves a mention for his input!

My sincere thanks to all my friends and colleagues who have instructed, helped and encouraged me to write this book, particularly Sylvia Loch, Teachers of Tomorrow Trust, Jaki Bell, Karen Croft, Dierdre Oddy, and Bridget Parry-James.

Lastly I must acknowledge Caroline Burt of J. A. Allen for having faith in me, Martin Diggle and Jane Lake for their expert advice, my mum, Jean Hansen, who has helped me with the illustrations and my partner Dougald Ballardie for spending hours behind the camera, (sometimes in adverse conditions!) taking many of the photographs for this book.

Introduction

Poles are not just for jumping. They make a very versatile training aid for all disciplines, which is of great benefit to both horse and rider. They help the rider improve accuracy and riding technique, and develop the horse's suppleness, strength, and obedience.

- In the school, ground poles can be used for a variety of exercises which make basic school work more interesting, challenging the ability of the rider by creating a degree of difficulty within the simplest of exercises.
- They help with the early training from the ground for the young horse, creating mental stimulation, for example, which helps to increase attention span. In-hand work and lungeing with the more experienced horse can also be enhanced by the exercises described in this book.
- Poles are a useful tool for the remedial training of horses who have developed problems in their behaviour, and also for those who need to develop a better way of going.
- Hacking becomes safer and more enjoyable on a well-trained horse who is used to unusual objects, and will go where you ask him! Simulating potentially tricky situations in the school will mean safer riding and can be a useful stepping stone for you both to help you deal with situations you would meet when riding out.
- Obstacle courses can be made as easy or difficult as you wish, with a bit of imaginative ground-pole use.
- If you are a dressage enthusiast you can use ground poles to outline different combinations of movements, improving accuracy and suppleness, especially if you are training on your own. Simple improvement of the gaits can be achieved, creating more athletic strides. The degree of difficulty achieved is determined by how the exercises are set out. The ambitious dressage rider, at any level, can get a lot out of the personal challenge of training their own horse to a higher standard.
- Equitation jumping is a combined competition of dressage and jumping, for which the training in this book would be extremely useful. Years ago, Prix Caprilli competitions were popular; they were designed to test both dressage movements and the jumping technique of both horse

and rider and included a few small jumps or cavalletti. A revival of this type of competition would be a very good test of correct training.

• Pole work improves jumping technique by helping to develop power, strength and rhythm, for example. Some of the exercises are designed to improve course riding, others to aid basic skills, and are applicable to both the inexperienced rider and the advanced rider wishing to fine-tune their jumping ability. The pole exercises in the jumping section can also be used when you progress to working over small jumps. A course of jumps is not necessary for the exercises described; however, once you have mastered the basics, the height of the jump is not the major factor when developing your technique. Once you have completed this section you should be proficient enough to tackle a course of show jumps and cross-country fences in good style and in a safe and efficient manner. At this point, you will need access to various jumping courses to continue your training.

• If your interest lies with eventing, you can practise basic jumping exercises, such as various angles of approach, and turning accurately and safely, by marking out with poles, or other suitable materials, various obstacles that you will come up against on a course. Become confident before venturing out beyond the security of the schooling area.

I hope you will find this book interesting and stimulating and that it encourages you to develop your own exercises, using the techniques shown, to further your individual riding ambitions.

Part I

Getting Started

Equipment

Most horse owners have limited budgets to work with, so the requirements for the exercises in this book have been kept to an affordable minimum. As with any training programme, the most important component is rider commitment, which no amount of money can buy! Starting a new training regime is a serious undertaking for both you and your horse. If you are less than 100 per cent committed, then you will not reap a 100 per cent result. Before starting this training programme, make sure that you are able to devote the additional training time, which is essential for long-term success.

First, you need a reasonably level area to ride in, which can range from an Olympic-sized arena, a sand school, or a quiet spot in a field. The going needs to be suitable for training, so clay, which has been baked to a brick-like surface or poached several inches deep, will not do. If in doubt, walk the ground yourself beforehand and try to imagine how the going will affect your horse's ability to do what you will be asking of him.

Setting out the poles on a good surface. The distance between these poles is about 1.5 m (5ft), a suitable gap to ride through. A rough guide is that the distance should be a long human stride, plus one foot's length.

Next, you will need a minimum of four long poles, planks or branches to mark out the exercises, although two poles will be enough in some circumstances. Failing that, most of the exercises can be marked out with plastic cones or plastic blocks. These can all be purchased relatively easily. Plastic barrels can be used, but they may need to be partially filled with sand to stop them blowing over in a strong wind and startling your horse. Old rubber feed bins or skips (manure baskets) that are past their best also have their uses as markers. Rubber buckets (minus handles), placed upside-down, are better than plastic ones, as they are less likely to tip over.

A selection of useful equipment: plastic blocks, poles, cavalletti, and jump wings.

Cavalletti are a useful addition to pole work. Set at their lowest height, they can be used to improve the athleticism of your horse. You may, however, prefer to use poles supported on plastic blocks to raise them off the ground. With blocks, it is possible to raise one end of the pole instead of both should you wish.

Basic Pole Arrangement

STAR-SHAPED ARRANGEMENT

For some exercises the poles should be laid out in a star shape. During these exercises, the space between the inner ends of the poles needs to be about 7 m (23ft), or seven average human strides.

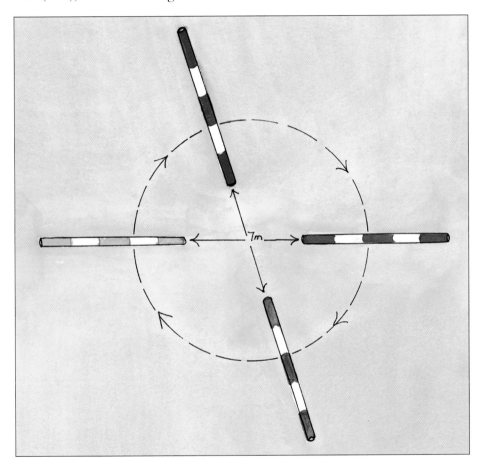

Four poles laid out in a star arrangement

PARALLEL POLES

Where the poles need to be set parallel to each other for you to work between them, they should be about 3 m (10ft) apart.

POLES SIMULATING A COURSE OF JUMPS

For some transition work, the poles should be set out around the schooling area so that you can ride from one to the other without any impossibly sharp turns, in the same way as you would plan a course of jumps.

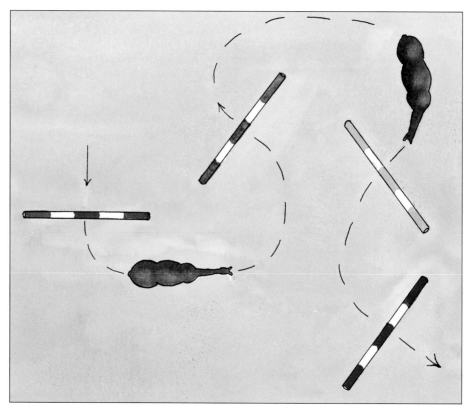

Poles laid out to simulate a course of jumps.

Substituting Markers for Poles

If you are using plastic cones or blocks, then place one at either end of where a pole would be or, if you have enough, mark them out in parallel lines if you are riding between them. Old, clean, empty paint tins, with the lids securely on, also make excellent markers. A friend of mine actually used full tins of dog food as markers, leaving her dog totally confused about why his dinner was out in the field, so he sat sulking on the sidelines all morning!

Plastic cones marking out an exercise.

Safety First

The Riding Area

In an ideal world every rider would have access to a perfectly level school kitted out with all the accoutrements; the real world is rather different! Many riders need to train their horses in fields in less-than-perfect conditions. The following suggestions should help you to begin this training programme quickly and cost-effectively. Remember that safety is paramount: never use any materials which could injure you or your horse or which are inherently unsafe.

Branches or logs are a great substitute for poles if you remove the odd small twigs that might stick out and catch your horse on the leg. Rotten branches

Poles in good condition are safer to use than old, rotten ones that are likely to fracture if hit.

will break and splinter if hit, so take care when selecting them. Alternatively, plastic pipes are wonderfully light to handle, resistant to weather conditions and easy to store, making them ideal for long-term use. Choose plastic drainpipes that are not brittle and likely to shatter if hit. They need to be about 8-10 cm (3-4 in) in diameter. They are also easy to paint and can be used instead of coloured poles for the jumping exercises later on.

If you use rubber buckets for markers, it is best to remove the handles from them, in case the buckets get knocked over and you or your horse trips over them or gets a leg caught in them.

The riding area needs to be fairly even and level, but remember that your horse's sense of balance and self-preservation improve a great deal if he can cope with slightly uneven or sloping ground and not only working in an arena. Many competitions, both dressage and jumping, are held in fields and are not necessarily beautifully manicured! Providing that it is not dangerously boggy or rocky and you do not work him on the side of a mountain, almost any field, or arena will do. An enclosed area is best in case you fall off or let go of your horse (risking possible injury if you are schooling near a busy road) and at least then you will not have to walk miles to find him!

Tack

While cleaning tack can be a chore, it is vital that your tack is in excellent condition, with all of the stitching, buckles and hooks intact and working perfectly. The sight of Mark Todd whizzing around Burghley with one stirrup is inspiring, but all riders risk injury if their tack breaks. Your tack does not have to be new but it should be well cared for.

A well-fitting, well-cared-for saddle is essential for safety and comfort.

Horse and Rider Fitness and Wellbeing

Your horse's shoeing is very important. Always have regular appointments with your farrier. Even if you work your horse without shoes, it is important to keep his feet balanced and in good condition. This will help your horse's way of going and prevent him stumbling or tripping. His gaits can be affected by poor shoeing, so if you find any irregularities in your horse's way of going, or his stride does not improve with work, discuss this with your farrier and/or vet.

It is also essential to get your horse's teeth checked on a regular basis. Wolf teeth can lead to bitting problems and sharp teeth can cause mouth ulcers and other problems which will affect your horse's willingness to have a bit in his mouth. Bad teeth can also affect your horse's ability to chew and digest his food and, in some instances, lead to colic. The most practical solution is to arrange a dental check with your vet at the same time as your horse's yearly flu booster. If problems appear under saddle when you are training your horse – particularly if he becomes agitated about the rein contact – the first thing to do is get his teeth checked. If his teeth are OK or if problems persist after rasping, you might need to change the bit or noseband. Bear in mind that many problems with the way a horse uses his back stem from uncomfortable teeth, an incorrectly fitting saddle, foot problems or simply poor riding.

In some cases, a previous accident or fall might have caused a problem, which only becomes apparent once your horse has been worked properly over a period of time. Muscle problems can go undetected for a long time because horses learn to carry themselves in a particular way to protect the muscles. Imagine that you have a sore shoulder and that you start to carry your shoulders at different levels because it is more comfortable, you would then need to correct your posture by sitting up straight, with a possible visit to the chiropractor to even you up again. The best thing you can do for your horse is to learn how to train him correctly to prevent injury and incorrect muscle development, though he might need treatment by your vet and physiotherapist to overcome a long-term problem. Consult your vet if you are worried.

Always work sensibly according to your horse's state of fitness. Begin all new exercises in walk to familiarize him with the requirements and to warm up his muscles (and yours) before proceeding further. Pole work once or twice a week is a valuable addition to your horse's regime because it can enhance normal exercises and improve their effectiveness. However, it is important to keep your horse fit and well. As his fitness increases, you will need to increase his hard feed and hay rations accordingly to help him build muscle. In other words, it is body building for your horse! Ensure that you are fit enough to train your horse. Correct riding requires good muscle tone and stamina. There is no point in getting your horse fit if you are worn out after ten minutes. You need strength to maintain your position in the saddle, not for strong aids.

Wear appropriate clothing when training your horse, particularly youngsters. When lungeing or leading, wear stout sensible footwear. Trainers, Sneakers or shoes with loose laces are not a good idea because the soft material will not protect your feet if you get trodden on and, unless you are very good with knots, they have a habit of coming undone at the wrong moment. Always wear gloves to protect your hands when riding or handling your horse, especially if he is young or if you are training an unknown horse. It is always wise to wear a crash hat when working the horse from the ground, particularly if there is a chance that the horse is dangerous or panicky in any way. Hooves can fly very quickly in tricky situations; your safety must be paramount.

Take sensible precautions when moving equipment around and generally handling your horse. Your movements should always be careful and watchful, even when you are in his stable. I know someone who suffered a cracked rib because she let her youngster barge in to her as they both walked out of his stable. Watching your horse's behaviour and being aware of what is going on around you (such as noticing the combine harvester in the next field heading your way) enables you to take calm, preventative measures without panicking your horse, helping you both to train safely.

Tack and Equipment

It is best to keep tack simple when trying to obtain the most benefit from training your horse using pole work. It is worth taking time to learn correct training techniques than to go for a quick fix which could have a disastrous long-term effect on your horse.

Bits

A snaffle bridle is best and I find the loose-ring, double-jointed continental training bits with a rounded lozenge are wonderfully comfortable for the horse and sit well in the mouth. They are expensive, but worth every penny. Quite often a horse who is fussy in his mouth settles very well with one of these, but a stainless steel, double-jointed mouthpiece (or French link) is also quite acceptable. Some horses may not be comfortable with the flat central link, and may find stainless steel rather cold. Sometimes a simple straight bar bit does the trick. These can be made of many different materials these days, so it may be a question of trial and error to find which suits you both the best.

If your horse is unsteady in his head carriage and fiddles around, you might find that he goes better in an eggbutt snaffle or a Fulmer snaffle. They both have a thick, firm part where the mouthpiece joins the rings, giving stability to the bit. The Fulmer snaffle is loose ringed, but the long cheeks on the mouthpiece have the same non-pinch style of the eggbutt. If your horse tends to set his jaw, a loose-ring snaffle is best, as it allows movement of the bit in the horse's mouth and encourages chewing and a relaxed tongue.

Make sure that whichever bit you choose, the mouthpiece is relatively thick which makes it mild. However, if your horse has a fleshy mouth and small lips, you must make sure that a thick mouthpiece is not too much of a mouthful for him.

Nosebands

A noseband can be used to encourage your horse to keep a relaxed and straight jaw. A horse may be quiet in his mouth without a noseband right from the start if he is extremely light and sensitive, but more usually he will benefit from a well-fitted noseband.

CAVESSON NOSEBAND

The cavesson is the simplest noseband. It should be fitted so that two fingers can be inserted between the noseband and the front of the nose bone. It should lie around the nose, equidistant between the cheekbones and the corners of the mouth. The noseband discourages the horse from opening his mouth too wide, i.e. to the point where he yaws and bears down against the bit. Horses who do this have learnt that they can pull the rider out of position by doing so, and it can be most disconcerting for the rider. Do bear in mind that this habit could be caused by incorrect riding, weakness in the horse, or other physical factors, such as teeth problems. A cavesson noseband is the only noseband that should be used in conjunction with a double bridle, since any other pattern will interfere with the action of the bits.

DROP NOSEBAND

A drop noseband fits lower around the nose than a cavesson, passing under the rings of the bit to prevent the horse from opening his mouth too far (rather than clamping it shut) and to help keep the jaw straight. A drop noseband encourages the horse to keep his tongue quiet and to chew on the bit. However, it is important that this noseband is not done up too tightly, because this will cause tension in the mouth. If, on the other hand, it is too loose and ineffective, you might as well use a cavesson. Quite often, once the horse has become accustomed to keeping a straight, steady contact with the bit via the drop noseband, you can either revert to a cavesson with no problems or go without a noseband altogether, though you may feel your horse is undressed if you are not used to riding like this.

FLASH NOSEBAND

A flash noseband combines both the cavesson and the drop nosebands. It is a stronger noseband than the drop and can be useful if your horse has learnt the knack of crossing and setting his jaw. Many horses go well in a flash because it encourages the whole jaw to remain straight and steady. This noseband should be fitted so that one finger fits between the cavesson part and the nose, and one finger between the drop strap and the chin groove, but the cavesson must be secure enough so that it does not sag down with the drop part fastened. Fasten the cavesson before the drop to prevent this happening. If the flash is too tight, it sets up tension in the contact with the bit and can often disguise a rider's poor use of the reins to an onlooker, because the horse cannot move his jaw. The flash noseband should not be used in this way. Again, once this noseband has done its job, revert to a simple cavesson.

The Double Bridle

Progression to a double bridle is not necessary for the exercises in this book, but it deserves a mention as a later development in your training regime. Over time, which could mean one to two years, depending on your progress, once your horse works well in a snaffle in all gaits and his self-carriage and outline are well established, you may decide to introduce the double bridle. Riding in a double once a week or so should be sufficient, continuing your training mainly in a snaffle. You must be secure in your seat and proficient in your aiding to proceed to a double bridle. It is rather like being promoted at work, and something to aspire to! The bridoon is used as a snaffle and the curb bit

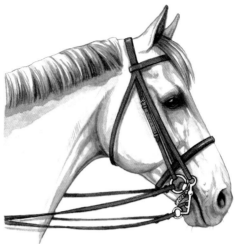

A snaffle bridle with a continental training bit and a flash noseband.

A double bridle with cavesson noseband.

encourages flexion at the poll, and softness in the jaw. Finesse is required to appreciate the fine control that these two bits give.

The bridoon is a small snaffle bit and comes in various forms. A single-jointed, loose-ring bridoon is common, though double-jointed versions are available.

The curb bit is available in many forms, but choose either a sliding mouthpiece for horses that need encouragement to chew, or a fixed mouthpiece for stability, in the same way that you selected your snaffle bit. Different metals are used, some warmer to the horse's mouth than steel.

The curb chain must be fitted correctly so that the arms of the curb only move back to a 45-degree angle with the mouth when taking a contact with the rein. If it is too long, the arms of the bit will swing round too far and exert a great pressure on the bars of the mouth, pressing the mouthpiece into the tongue. If it is too short, too much poll pressure is exerted which causes tension in the horse's jaw. Only use a cavesson noseband with a double bridle, otherwise the bit action will be interfered with, causing much tension in the horse's mouth.

Saddles

While a general-purpose saddle is fine for the work outlined in this book, you may prefer a dressage saddle or a jumping saddle if you decide to specialize and take up either of these disciplines seriously. A dressage saddle encourages a longer, more vertical leg position with a close contact through the thigh and calf, while a jumping saddle allows you to ride with your thigh close to the knee rolls in front of your body, creating a very secure seat for jumping.

A qualified master saddler should check your saddle at least annually; youngsters and older horses benefit from more frequent checks. Your horse's muscles will develop as he becomes fitter, changing both his shape and his self-carriage. The most important thing about the saddle is that it must fit both you and your horse. Regular safety checks on its fitting and the state of the stitching should be part of your normal routine when cleaning your tack. Many books have been devoted to the art of saddle fitting; anyone starting a serious training programme should ensure that their saddle fits their horse.

Quite often, faulty saddle fitting only becomes more apparent once you are riding your horse correctly. Problems can frequently go undetected. How many of us can feel if the horse is truly straight, supple through his back and comfortable in his work? If there is a problem, once you ask the horse to work absolutely correctly, he suddenly becomes tense or tight and resists the bit. This does not necessarily mean that you have given a wrong aid; it may mean that a problem is being uncovered which previously went undetected. If this happens, get your saddle checked straight away.

The seat of your saddle should allow you to sit upright without being tipped forward or back. Often, as the horse's shoulder muscles become more developed, the saddle can be tipped back and, as his loin muscles develop, it can be tipped forward. Check the way your saddle sits on the horse every few months and remember that it may need checking sooner if your horse develops quickly. If the saddle is too narrow, your horse's shoulder movement will be restricted. Your horse might tell you that his saddle is too narrow by refusing to work in a rounded outline, as a narrow saddle will exacerbate the problem. If the saddle is too wide, the problem will be rather more obvious: you and the saddle will be slipping around!

Gadgets

There is no quick fix or magic formula for training a horse, but people increasingly want quick results and resort to using gadgets which is not a good idea at all. Gadgets do not encourage the rider to develop a correct seat and aids, and certainly do not promote correct outline, balance and muscle development in the horse. More often than not, gadgets have a detrimental effect on training and it can take several months to correct the problems that they can cause.

There are many gadgets and training aids on the market and I have to say that I only use, and approve of, two, for *lungeing only*: the chambon and side reins. These must be correctly fitted and their use understood and judiciously applied. These two items are explained further on pages 30–31. There should be, however, no need for supplementary reins, etc., with the ridden training programme outlined in this book, as the horse's muscles should be developing correctly over several months to give a long-term solution to the most common problems.

Basic Principles of Lungeing

The horse should be considered an athlete. Successful athletes train, tune up their muscles and get ultra-fit. As a result, they look fit, happy and healthy, have good posture and exude a sense of wellbeing. Similarly, if a horse is to be worked properly, he must be trained in a way that makes him fit, happy and healthy.

The most fundamental training requirement is to be able to work your horse on the lunge. When lungeing the horse, you have an opportunity to observe the way in which he moves and to study his outline and it is advisable to perfect your lungeing technique before attempting to lunge over poles. Pole work on the lunge is explained on page 69. The advantages of lungeing are:

• establishing a rapport with your horse
• being able to see him work from the ground
• he learns to balance himself without the hindrance of a rider
• bending and transitions can be established and improved
• gaits are developed

Lungeing is an excellent foundation for future training and ridden work. It is easy to gauge a horse's fitness level from his shape and musculature, the way he moves and by his posture, or self-carriage. When people refer to the outline of the horse, they mean the shape in which he moves, which is an indication of whether his training is correct or not. Outline is explained further on page 67.

Without any rein contact at all, a novice horse will probably look at his surroundings and either carry his head fairly high, or he may stretch his neck out flat, poking his nose forward. As he relaxes, he should hopefully begin to stretch down towards the ground. He will find it difficult to remain on an evenly shaped circle, which results in him either falling in or pulling away from you. In order to develop the outline in a way which helps him balance, bend and stretch, the horse needs to understand rein contact. This does not mean short cuts and gadgets, it means taking time to develop your horse's muscles correctly. Imagine going to the gym and aimlessly having a go at the various weight machines without understanding how you should use your body. The result could easily be under- or over-developed muscles, incorrect posture or an injury. It is the same with your horse; if he is worked incorrectly over time, his development will be impaired and he will lose the ability to work normally because of physical impediments.

Lungeing Equipment

You will need:
• snaffle bridle
• lunge cavesson
• long lunge line
• gloves
• sensible footwear (many boots come with protective toe caps)
• roller (surcingle) or saddle
• brushing boots
• chambon
• side reins
• extra-long lunge whip

USING THE EQUIPMENT
It is simple; first tack up your horse. With the **bridle**, either take the reins off so that they do not get in the way, or twist them together under the horse's jaw and secure them by passing the throatlatch between the reins. If you are using a **lunge cavesson**, fit it over the bridle (it might be best to remove the noseband from the bridle as it may get in the way of the cavesson nosepiece). Make sure that it is securely fitted to avoid it being pulled to one side when you are lungeing. If you are learning to lunge, and the horse is well behaved, it is best to use the cavesson with the lunge line

attached to the centre ring. This will save you having to detach the line as you change direction, and you will learn your lungeing skills without accidentally catching the horse with the bit. It is better to work from the cavesson if you can but if you have a good understanding of contact there may be instances when you will find it beneficial to also work your horse from the bridle as you would when riding him. Take care to be subtle, however, as the horse can draw his tongue back in his mouth if he becomes tense. There are attachments available which clip onto each bit ring, linking them together under the chin, to which you can attach a lunge line.

Choose a **lunge line** with a good hand loop and notches, which make it easier to keep the line a constant length and maintain a better grip than with a smooth line. A soft line is more comfortable to hold than a stiff webbing one. Always wear **gloves**. It is a good idea to wear gloves that are a little bit too big, so that they come off easily if you get your hand caught up in the line. Put your hand through the loop and coil the line in evenly so that it pays out easily. Should your horse try to make a run for it, let out the line so he is on a large circle and with firm tugs, holding the loop, re-establish control, re-coiling the line as he settles down. Do not try to hang on to him on a tight circle. This will cause him to panic. Breaking away is usually a result of poor lungeing technique, with the handler not being quick enough to act with firm tugs on the line. If you pull, your horse will most certainly pull away from you. Wear **sensible footwear** (see list of equipment on page 28) to avoid tripping up. It is not a lot of fun being dragged about on your knees by a wilful horse!

If you are using a **roller** (surcingle), use a pad underneath it for comfort and also to prevent rubbing and make sure that it is securely fastened. Choose a roller with rings on the sides for the attachment of the side reins. The side reins need to be the correct height on the saddle or roller. Too high causes a hollow outline, while if they are too low, the horse will over-bend and look at his knees. The rings on the roller need to be about halfway up the horse's sides. If using a **saddle**, make sure that your girth is tight enough to prevent the saddle being pulled forward. A saddle pad or numnah is recommended because your horse will work better is he is comfortable. If your horse is unfit and has very soft skin, use an elasticated girth to avoid chafing. Run the stirrups up and secure the leathers through their keepers on the saddle flaps if you want them out of the way.

If your horse is unbalanced or has a tendency to brush, **brushing boots** will prevent him from catching himself on his fetlocks as he moves. A straight-moving, well-balanced horse should not injure himself, but there is always the chance he will have a 'funny five minutes' and do something unexpected!

In order to help your horse learn to stretch correctly down to the ground, a **chambon** is the kindest and simplest aid to use. It enables the horse to stretch down in an unrestricted manner, while preventing him from raising his head and neck too high, and it encourages him to use his back and neck muscles correctly while stopping him from using the underside muscles on his neck, which are the ones horses use to fix their necks against the rider's hand. A chambon teaches the horse to work with a supple back with his haunches starting to take weight and with the hind legs coming forward under the body. If correctly fitted, the chambon is totally loose when the horse stretches down and chews on the bit with a relaxed jaw. A chambon also helps a horse to develop a good rhythm, as he cannot run against the rein. He also has to learn to balance on all four legs – much like being in four-wheel drive!

A young horse working in a chambon. Note the upper muscles of the neck being used, and the stomach muscles tucking the pelvis under, giving a rounded top line and resulting in the inside hind leg stepping under the body.

Once your horse can stretch down correctly, a pair of **side reins** will teach him to reach forward toward the bit and work in a round outline. Elasticated side reins are a good idea if you are both inexperienced, or if you have a nervous horse who tends to panic. However, plain side reins are better for establishing a steady contact with most horses, as they learn to be quiet and work with a consistent head carriage. Bossy horses tend to play and pull at the elastic side reins and then tend to do the same thing when they are ridden, giving the rider a hard time.

Fix side reins level with the bottom of the saddle flaps: if you go any higher, the horse will tend to hollow his back in the beginning. They should be fitted so that the horse looks as he would if you were riding him in a correct outline for his particular stage of training. Once the horse has the confidence to stretch down in this way, and trusts the bit in his mouth, he needs to learn how to work into a contact as though under saddle. Be aware that your horse needs to be worked correctly with good gaits to prevent over-bending. If the side reins are too short, the horse will be tense and tuck his chin in. If they are too long, they will have no effect and the horse will not develop his top line; instead, he may work with a hollow back and disengaged hind legs. If your horse has never worn side reins before, lunge him quietly with just the outside one on at first. Attach the lunge line either to the inside ring on the cavesson, or to the inside bit ring so that you can maintain a contact, acting as the inside rein. If all goes well, then attach the other side rein on the inside and lunge normally.

A novice horse reaching forward to accept the contact with the bit in plain side reins in a relaxed, rounded outline. To encourage this, the side reins are fixed just below the saddle flaps.

It takes a lot of practice to learn to work a horse correctly on the lunge, but it is far better to take the time to train him and develop correct muscles, rather than to rush the process and end up with an unhappy, badly developed horse. Remember that it takes about three months to alter the shape of a horse and that all training has the sole long-term objective of creating an athletic, happy horse. Any problems with outline when under saddle are best corrected by taking time and care on the lunge and being observant. The horse can then work through his problems of balance and self-carriage without the rider and learn to recognize and understand your aids. You will both be safe and the lungeing process will develop a respectful rapport between you.

How to Begin

Initially, just go for a walk. Lead your horse around the school in a relaxed manner. He should walk, halt and turn when you do. Do not look at him; instead, walk purposefully forward and expect him to come, too. You might have to tap him behind with your lunge whip to encourage him (keep the lash in your hand, not dragging along behind). Once he is listening to you, ask him to halt and walk on again. If he tries to barge in to you, push him away with your elbow. If he does not want to stop, give a good tug on the line which should be attached to the cavesson. Keep a relaxed wrist when you do this, so that the line jangles the cavesson ring rather than jerking on it sharply. Be as firm to him as he is to you. If you have a sensitive horse, be tactful and behave in a quiet and gentle manner. If you have a bullish character be bossy! Once he will walk and halt nicely for you, you are ready for your first lunge session.

Never warm your horse up with the side reins or chambon on; he must warm up before they are used. When you walk in to the school, or your training area, step back to the horse's side, and point the whip at his hocks. You should now be facing the horse's belly, with the lunge line in the hand nearest the horse's head. The horse, whip and lunge line make a triangle with you at the apex. Let the line out and ask him to trot. Give a preparatory half-halt on the line (small tug) and hold it taut so that it is in a straight line to the horse. If the line is loose, he will probably just speed up in walk and will not understand that you want a transition.

Lungeing is quite an individual thing and each horse has key words he picks up. Unless another person knows your commands, they will have a problem lungeing your horse. Keep your horse interested in his work by using your voice in an encouraging way, but do not chat aimlessly at him. Horses can learn word commands, so if you are consistent in the words that you use, he will learn your 'language'.

Use your voice and give a clear, assertive command to trot. If you do not say it with conviction, he will know you do not really mean it, and wander aimlessly around! There is no need to yell at him, though. At the same time, aim your whip in a sweeping movement towards his hocks as a substitute for your leg aid when on board. A flick on his thigh with the end of the whip may be necessary if he is reluctant to go into trot. Brandishing it in the air like a weapon may alarm him, and cracking it on the ground just makes a noise. You may flatten the odd beetle doing this but your horse will not understand what you mean! Then, decrease the size of the circle with small tugs on the line to ask him to walk again. Combine this with a voice aid to walk. Again, a calm but assertive manner should be sufficient. If your horse is not listening, a lot of quick transitions will wake him up; if he is too fizzy, settle him by slowing the rhythm in trot either by making the circle slightly smaller with half-halts on the line, or say a word such as 'steady' as well as using half-halts, until he is relaxed. For the young horse, this would be enough for the first few sessions.

Five minutes warm up is adequate for less fit horses, and up to ten minutes for fitter horses. At this stage, you can attach the chambon or the side reins as you wish. Send your horse off in trot again. With the chambon, you want him to stretch down as far as he can. As he stretches, look at his back muscles. They should be working, especially behind the saddle in his loin area. His haunches should look as though they are tucking under and his hind legs should reach further under his belly than normal.

Attach the side reins so that he looks as though he is 'on the bit', i.e. with his nose a little in front of the vertical for a young horse, progressing to vertical for an experienced horse. Send him off in a good working trot so that he has to put a bit of effort into it! Transitions are useful to encourage him to be obedient, while increasing and decreasing the size of circle will help him to become more supple. The lunge whip is a substitute for your leg aids, so use it accordingly.

A more advanced horse working in side reins with good impulsion in his trot.

Lunge for a minimum of ten minutes and a maximum of half an hour. The length of time depends on the fitness of the horse and also if you intend to ride him afterwards. He would need a short session if further work were to follow. Watch your horse to gauge his fitness level. If he is puffing like a train after five minutes, he is not very fit! You then need to gradually build up the frequency and length of the lunge sessions over three to four weeks. A horse who is coping well with being lunged will become warmer and breath more quickly without becoming stressed. If he is sweating profusely and flaring his nostrils, then you have overdone it

Finish your session with a short period without the side reins or chambon; it is very important that you give your horse this opportunity to relax and recover from lungeing, which is quite hard work for him. You can go for another walk around at the end.

Part II

Basic Training for the Novice or Young Horse

In-hand Work

Pole work is a valuable part of any young horse's education. Young horses have a short attention span and low energy levels, so each lesson needs to be brief and focused.

Once you are able to lead your horse in hand, he then needs to learn to follow you and trust your commands.

Always wear gloves to protect your hands, give a better grip on the lead rope and prevent rope burns when working with youngsters. Stout shoes or boots, which protect your feet from rampant hooves, are also an excellent idea. I know someone who wears his motorbike leathers when handling youngsters for the first few times, because they have padding in all of the right places, including shin pads! It is also advisable to wear a crash cap when handling horses from the ground, especially if you have an unruly pupil or if you have a relatively new horse who you are not quite sure of. Your safety is important, particularly during a horse's early training stages when temper tantrums can come fast and furious.

Ensure that you are in a safe environment like a school or some sort of enclosed area. Choose a quiet time at the yard and reasonable weather. It is no fun hanging on to a precocious two-year-old if the horse is easily upset or spooked by things such as tractors, other horses moving around or thunder and lightning.

Lead your horse from a lunge cavesson, stout headcollar, or a Be Nice halter using a new lead rope (old ones have a habit of breaking at exactly the wrong moment) or a lunge line in good condition.

How to Begin

Begin by leading your horse around the edge of the schooling area, practising walk and halt transitions as you go. Then change direction and repeat on the other rein. Get used to leading from either side but it is best to be on the inside as you go around the school, to stop you from getting squashed against the fence! This will probably take two or three sessions to establish, but stick with it. Be prepared for spookiness, temper and a positive lack of attention. Keep the first few sessions short and just long enough so that your horse understands you, but not so long that he gets stressed or tired. You might need to do two short sessions each day (five minutes) rather than one longer one if this is practical. Remember that it is the quality of what you achieve when training your horse, not the quantity. If you get what you want in five or ten minutes, congratulate your horse (and yourself) on a successful session and finish on a positive note. Similarly, if you are not getting anywhere, do not continue the same negative cycle for an hour, because you will be giving your horse a bad schooling session.

Use your voice in a calm, authoritative manner. Carry a schooling whip to help with your aids if necessary. The horse should move when you do and stop with you. You may have to give a short tug on the rope the first few times and then your horse should get the idea and follow you. Try to stay by his shoulder at all times. If your horse tries to shoot off, stand firmly in front of his shoulder and hold your ground physically and mentally. Learn to plant yourself on the spot to prevent this happening; you will need to do this throughout his training programme!

Keep a firm grip on the lead rope without tensing up. When your horse is walking well, relax your hand on the line, but be ready to be firm should you need to. Stop walking and, without looking behind you, expect your horse to halt with you. If he tries to walk past you, stand your ground and give a firm half-halt on the rope. He must learn to respond to you stopping. If he turns in on you (a favourite trick with intelligent youngsters), place your elbow firmly against his neck and push him away from you. Keep your feet out of the way – turning in is frequently accompanied by fancy hoofwork!

Try to handle a young horse in a calm, relaxed manner at all times, even when he becomes fractious or downright bolshy. Be firm enough to stand your ground, be authoritative, but never be angry or nervous. This is an incredibly difficult balance to achieve and even more so if you are putting pressure on yourself to succeed with training your own horse. If you are at all worried about your horse, get some help from someone who is not fazed by his behaviour and who can help you through the difficult times.

Young horses take time to learn self-control, so it is important to be understanding and patient. Tough love might be an apt approach. As much as you want your horse to love you, he must understand that you mean what you say. This is as much for your own safety as his training. If he learns to do what you expect *at the first time of asking* you will be happy to praise him. If, on the other hand, he slams you into a fence post because he has seen a donkey in the next field who looks far more interesting, then a bit of respect has to be established pretty smartly! Your tone of voice needs to be stern, not angry (this takes some practice!) and stronger tugs on your lead rope/lunge line will be necessary. He must realize that you are still attached to him, otherwise you risk being dragged about to visit said donkey against your wishes!

As you progress, work up to leading the horse in trot for short spells, making transitions from walk to trot. This exercise helps to improve the horse's balance.

Progressing to Poles

Once you have established the rules of leading, and your horse starts to respect and trust you, try walking over individual poles. The poles will add an intellectual challenge to your horse's training and give him something new to focus on. Lay single random poles around the school. Lead your horse around and over them. Walk purposefully forward; your horse should follow you. Occasionally walk straight over the poles, and then halt in front of each one before proceeding. By doing this, your horse learns that

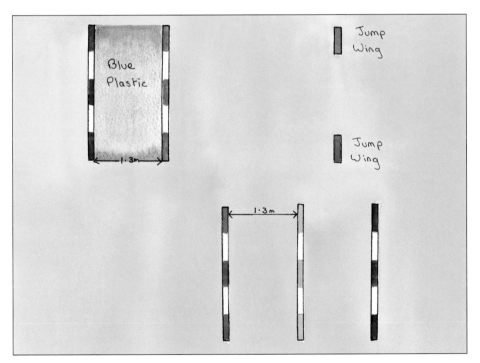

A simple obstacle course giving various options of going over a sequence of poles, around wings, and over a sheet of plastic, which should be secured on the ground with heavy poles.

Building confidence and trust with a young horse working in hand using various obstacles for added interest.

he should not charge over a pole every time he sees one. Practise weaving in and out of the poles and walking alongside a line of poles. This is a good exercise if you hope to do dressage competitions with your horse because it teaches him to keep within the marker boards that mark out the arena.

Set out jump wings or something suitable to lead him around and in between. Once he is beginning to trust you, introduce something more challenging, such as a sheet of plastic secured with poles so that it does not move or get blown by the wind. Walking with your horse will give him confidence with these exercises and encourage him to have a flexible approach.

A SEQUENCE OF POLES

The next progression is to tackle a sequence of poles. Lie the poles at about 6 m (19½ ft)apart, which is a fairly wide spacing. This gives you the necessary time and space in which to make corrections and enables you to halt or circle away if needed. After a few sessions, gradually bring the poles closer together until they are a walk stride apart (0.8 m or 2½ ft which is a small stride for most people). Once you and your horse can walk over the poles, progress to trotting over them. Set them at a distance of 1.3 m (4 ft), generally one big stride plus a foot's length. The distances given are approximate and can vary from horse to horse according to stride length. You will need to be fairly fit for this, as a fair bit of running is involved! If your horse tries to go too fast for you, steady him with clear tugs on the line. Release the rope in between the aids so that your horse understands when he has responded correctly and done well. Make sure that you reward your horse as soon as he has done well.

Finish the session once you have managed each exercise two or three times correctly and always finish on a good note. If you try something too difficult for your horse and he gets confused or agitated, go back to an earlier exercise that he has done well, so that he feels confident at the end of the lesson and is keen to re-enter the school for a positive training session.

Mounting and Dismounting

There is an art to mounting and dismounting which all riders should perfect. If done well, you and your horse should appear effortlessly elegant; if badly executed, you can, over time, cause problems with your horse's back and confidence and probably harm your saddle.

With a young horse, it is always advisable to have a helper on hand when mounting your horse for the first few times, because this is a crucial stage in your horse's development. When training your horse to be mounted, he must first of all learn to stand still. This sounds obvious, but it is very common to come across horses who fidget when mounted, even when they are older and wiser. Whether you are competing at an event, out hacking or at home in your arena, you need to be able to mount and dismount quickly and safely.

Choose a calm day for your first mounting lesson and a quiet time at the yard when distractions will be at a minimum. There is nothing worse than trying to mount a young horse in a thunderstorm or when heavy farm machinery is on the move. Lunge your horse first so he will not be tempted to hot up and to ensure that he is listening to you. He should not, however, be worn out because if he is tired he will not be responsive. Remember that young horses have a short attention span and low energy levels, so keep each lesson brief and focused.

Lay two poles parallel to each other like railroad tracks. The poles should be wide enough apart to allow the horse to stand between them facing one of the open ends. Lead the horse between the poles and halt. When he stands still nicely, praise him. Walk straight on in a calm and controlled manner and repeat this exercise a few times until he is relaxed when standing. If the exercise is successful, this will be enough for your first session.

If your horse has a problem with this exercise and walks off, lay a third pole on the ground so that it lies across the ends of the other two, forming three sides of a box. This exercise requires an assistant. This should act as a deterrent and give him something new to think about. This is an excellent strategy for dealing with intelligent and inquisitive young horses. When you are ready to move forward, your assistant needs to move one end of the pole around to allow you and the horse to walk through. The effect should be like going through an open door. Do make sure that your assistant is well out of the way before you move forward! Repeat this process again the next day. If the session goes well, repeat the exercise next time without the pole across the front of the box.

Once you have established a good halt, stand and walk, add a mounting block to the equation. For safety's sake, use materials which you know are durable and which can easily bear your weight, and withstand a knock or kick by your horse.

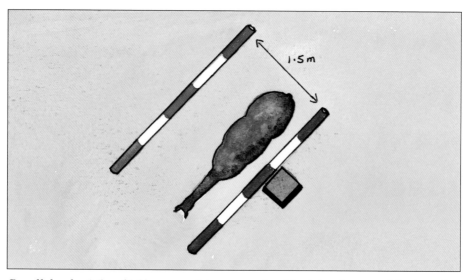

Parallel poles 1.5 m (5 ft) apart with a mounting block in place outside the poles.

Lead your saddled horse between the poles with the stirrups hanging by his sides in preparation for mounting. First, hold the left stirrup and lean on it, putting weight on it. Next, gently flap the leather against the saddle to make a noise. Try not to scare your horse, but remember that if he is used to a bit of noise and movement, he will not be alarmed when you get on board with your foot in the stirrup.

Mounting

Ask your assistant to stand on the offside of the horse and to hold the offside stirrup and the rein. You need a calm, confident assistant, since your horse will quickly pick up any signs of nervousness or fear and react accordingly.

Before you mount your horse for the first time, it is wise to stand him by your mounting block during the preceding few training sessions to get him used to you being above him. (Grooming him while you are standing on a box will also familiarize him with this.) Get your assistant to give you a leg up and lean carefully over the saddle, taking care to gently ease yourself on to your stomach over the saddle. Once your horse is used to this, your assistant can lead him forward a few steps at a time so he is becoming accustomed to your weight on his back. If you feel your horse tensing up, immediately stop and slide quietly to the ground. Your assistant can lead him around so he relaxes, then return to the mounting block, and repeat.

Standing on the mounting block, place your left foot in the left stirrup. It might be less alarming for your horse if you face forward when doing this. Because all of this is new, a youngster might take a step or two forward and it is much easier to quickly swing up into the saddle if you are facing forward. This position also allows you to see his expression and pre-empt his reactions. (A friend of mine tore the ligaments in her left knee when mounting a young horse facing backwards. The horse moved suddenly forward, and she could not turn to mount, consequently her knee was violently wrenched.) Pay particularly close attention to his ears: if he puts his ears flat back when you put your foot in the stirrup, keep your foot quietly there and reassure him. Stay put until he relaxes, then remove your foot and praise him. This is a major step in your horse's education and this might be as far as you get during this session. If he becomes overly stressed when your foot is in the stirrup, quietly remove it. Remain standing on the mounting block and reassure him. If he relaxes, try again. If he does not relax, repeat the first exercise of leading him between the poles and halting. Always go back a stage if your horse becomes at all tense or agitated.

Once you can put weight on your left foot, press on to the stirrup as though you are going to mount. If this is successful, ease yourself on to the saddle on your stomach. Leave your right leg hanging above the mounting block so that you can easily step down again if necessary. Your assistant should still be standing there holding the horse. When you can stay on your stomach without the horse becoming tense, ask your assistant to lead you around in a circle, returning between the two poles to dismount again. Praise your horse for another good session. Next time, you should be able to mount slowly astride. Stay very calm and make all of your movements easy and deliberate. Avoid thumping into the saddle at all costs. The sudden weight on your horse's back will alarm him and he will become afraid of having you on his back.

Your horse should now associate standing between the poles with halting for you to mount or dismount. Remove the nearside pole, but retain the mounting block. If at any time the horse attempts to walk away, calmly reposition him and start again. Once he is standing still with one pole there, remove it so that he is just standing by the mounting block. Your mission should now be accomplished, leaving you with a well-mannered horse who stands beautifully still for you. Once this lesson has been learned, you should have no future problems with mounting.

Mounting from a block with just one pole to keep the horse straight. The rider is facing forward to enable her to swing quickly and quietly into the saddle.

Dismounting

It can be alarming for a young horse if his rider takes both feet out of the stirrups and leaps off to dismount; he may well shoot forward, leaving his rider sitting on the ground, or stop dead! It is important to practise dismounting with your left foot still in the stirrup. The process is the reverse of mounting. With your assistant holding your horse, keep hold of the reins in your left hand, lean forward and slowly bring your right leg over the horse's back without touching him. Support your weight on your right hand on the pommel, then lean on your stomach on the saddle, removing your right hand to the back of the saddle. Ease yourself quietly off his back, without pulling the back of the saddle and keeping your left foot in the stirrup for support. When you have both legs on the left side, take your left foot out of the stirrup so that both legs are hanging freely and you do not get left with a foot in the stirrup. Dismount onto the block with your assistant holding your horse. If you are not near the block and have to make a dismount elsewhere in the school, ease yourself in the same way to the ground. Do make sure that the girth is still reasonably tight, especially on horses who are of a nervous disposition and who would be upset if the saddle moved. If you prefer jumping down to the ground by swinging your leg over the back of the horse, you can progress to this at a later stage, but take care not to accidentally knock your horse on his back as you come over. This could give you both a nasty surprise!

It is worth investing time in these early lessons and taking great care not to frighten your horse when mounting or dismounting. If things go wrong, it can take several months to restore his confidence.

Riding: Natural Aids and Position in the Saddle

Natural aids are the signals that you give to your horse with your body, i.e. your seat, legs, hands and voice. All of these can be used singly and in combination to achieve specific results. For example, when training a young or inexperienced horse, you would use all your aids simultaneously to ask your horse to halt, and then over time refine your aids so that he responds to an almost imperceptible seat aid. This is true for all supporting, collecting and driving aids used for dressage, show jumping, cross country and showing, plus activities like hacking and hunting. The art of riding is the same whether you are a serious competitor or simply enjoy hacking in the countryside. The aids work in conjunction with each other to have an overall effect over the horse's balance and how he moves in his gaits and performs the movements that you ask of him.

Seat Aids

The way you sit on your horse influences how your horse moves. A correct position in the saddle will enable you to give effective and clear instructions to your horse with the minimum of effort. Try to get in the habit of maintaining good posture in your daily life, such as sitting up straight when driving your car, and you will reap the benefits later in life!

Good posture in the saddle is the same as for when you are standing on the ground. You use the same postural muscles for both to control your balance. If you have a correct basic riding position, you will be sitting tall in the saddle and upright on your seat bones. By sitting in the central and deepest part of a well-balanced saddle, that fits both you and your horse, your weight should be distributed between your seat bones, crotch and your thighs giving stability to your pelvis. You should be able to feel the seat bones clearly. It is important to keep your seat muscles soft and not clenched, as you would then be sitting on a pad of muscle at the rear of your seat, instead of your seat bones. This would result in you tightening your tummy muscles too much and tucking your seat too far under.

In order to keep your pelvis upright you need to sit up straight, lifting up through the ribcage to stretch and tone both the stomach and lower back muscles. Stretch upwards from the waist, maintaining a natural arch in the small of your back. Lifting your chest will allow you to breathe deeply. Look up and ahead of you at all times. Your head is quite heavy so it can affect your balance quite dramatically! In a correct seat, you should not be a hindrance to the horse: your position must allow him to keep his back round and his pelvis tucked under, enabling him to bring his hind legs under his body to carry his weight evenly between his hind and forelegs. Balanced self-carriage allows your horse to work athletically, minimizing the risk of musculo-skeletal damage.

A rider in good balance produces an attentive, well-balanced horse, both mentally and physically.

Leg Aids

Your leg aids have various functions. In conjunction with your seat, the legs can remain hanging lightly, almost passively, against the horse's sides in a neutral position, which requires just enough muscle tone for them to remain in place. They must not grip on, or fall away from, the horse; instead, they should remain comfortably touching your horse with your toes and knees pointing forward. The hips must remain free from tension to help the legs to hang down (imagine your hip joints are well-lubricated). If your horse is well balanced, with his weight evenly on all four feet, you will just need enough muscle tone to maintain your position, because you will not need to alter the balance of the horse. If your horse is not balanced, he will need continual supportive aids from you to help him maintain his posture and work from behind. This is important and is explained further in Collection and Extension on page 86.

Badly positioned legs are ineffective and adversely affect your balance and the control of the horse.

Your thighs should be hanging down by the horse's sides and your feet need to be pointing forward with the balls of your feet resting on the stirrups. Stretch the back of your calves to lower your heels with flexed ankles. Try not to push your heels down, as this causes your feet to shoot forward and makes you sit back too far in the saddle.

The aids that you give with your calves should be in the form of nudges with the upper calf. Avoid trying to use your heels because this causes your feet and knees to stick out, lifting your thighs away from the saddle and rendering your seat insecure, as you no longer have the support of your thigh against the saddle. If the horse is going well, keep your legs quietly against his sides. He has to know the difference between when you are using your legs and when you are not. Nagging leg aids result in a switched-off horse!

Hand (Rein) Aids

Via the reins, your hands must maintain an elastic contact with both sides of the bit, something which should be effortless on a balanced horse. You can feel if he is uneven through his body and leaning on one side of the bit, or if he is straight and soft with an even contact on each rein. Conversely, he can tell from your hands whether you are frightened or calm, too dominant or too timid. Hand and rein aids should not be used more strongly than the rest of your body. Anything you do affects the horse as a whole, not just what you see in front of you. The tone of your upper arms should be enough to keep your elbows bent and in position by your sides. Your upper arm should be vertical. If your shoulders feel tight across the back and your hands are gripping the reins tightly, then you are tense rather than toned. Your hands should be carried just above the withers (not too high), keeping a straight line from your elbow to the bit (imagine holding a small tea-tray in front of you). Your horse's neck will be in a natural arch stretching forward from the withers to the bridle. Your hands and arms maintain this outline and should be soft and flexible when your horse gives you a soft feeling in his mouth and offer a firmer support momentarily if he needs it. The role of the rein aids in establishing/maintaining outline is important but subtle. The rein aids work in conjunction with the leg and seat aids, not just on their own. Learning to co-ordinate these aids takes time and practice. The tone of your seat, leg and rein aids should match. For example, if you are aware of your horse giving you a strong feel on the reins, this indicates that he is on his forehand and needs more support from your body and legs. If your reins feel too strong, immediately strengthen your position to match the strength of the reins by increasing the tone of your stomach and back muscles to prevent you being pulled out of position by your horse.

Close your thighs, knees and calves to hold your leg position. Your reins should feel instantly softer because you are now supporting the horse with your body rather than holding him up with the reins. This is in effect a half-halt, which is explained further on pages 75–76. Once you feel the horse soften, soften the tone of your reins, legs and body so that your horse learns to trust your contact and aiding and is not worried that you are going to hold him firmly for longer than one stride. If this happens, you have pulling reins, as opposed to supporting reins. The key is to be able to distinguish between a 'hold' and a 'pull'. It is fundamentally important to remember that you should not be holding your horse up with the reins: he should maintain his own balance. Riding a balanced horse is like being an invisible rider; you are surplus to requirements! Ultimately, a well-trained horse who is happy in his work should feel as though he is doing what you ask of his own volition.

Voice Aids

The way you speak to your horse can influence him greatly. Many horses can recognize simple words or expressions as well as picking up the tone of your voice. A calmly spoken 'steady' or 'stand' should have the desired effect rather than shouting, 'I said stop you b…..!' Screaming, yelling and getting yourself in a frenzy will only result in a frightened horse wondering what on earth you are doing. Use your voice with authority; never ever lose your temper. You must mean what you say. Being vague confuses your horse so develop clear, consistent instructions that are easy to remember and that he understands. My own horse recognizes, 'Do you want a sweet?' above all other phrases that I use. This works wonders in any circumstance.

POLE WORK TO HELP POSITION AND AIDS
Lay two poles parallel to each other and ride between them, concentrating on your own position in the saddle. Glance down at your hands and see if they are level with each other; if you are stronger one side than the other, your hands may unwittingly be uneven in height. Imagine a vertical line drawn down through your body. You should be symmetrical on both sides. You should be able to see if your knees are parallel, and should glimpse the tips of your toes below your knees.

Try to learn the feeling of being in a good position. Glance down at your hands to see if they are symmetrical. You should be able to see if your knees are parallel also.

Aids for Circles and Turns

There are a few basic things to remember about riding circles and turns. Foremost is the ability to keep the bend of the horse's body, around the circle. The inside aids are those to the inside of the bend of the horse and the outside aids are those on the outside of the bend of the horse.

To bend left, sit tall in the saddle keeping your pelvis upright to avoid collapsing to the inside. This helps to lift your horse's forehand, encouraging him to keep his weight on his hocks. (Do remember to breathe. Apart from keeping you alive, this can prevent tension creeping into your shoulder area!) Keep your weight slightly to the left, (sitting on your left seat bone) and down through your left leg, into the stirrup (without pushing it down) to anchor the bend. Your right (outside) leg is placed behind the girth to control the outside of the horse's body. Turn your upper body slightly to the left. By keeping your elbows by your sides as you turn, you will bring the horse's forehand around with you. The inside rein asks the horse to flex his head slightly to the left; this should be achieved by adjusting your upper body posture and moving the fingers on your left hand slightly. There should be no overt pulling of the inside rein. He should bend evenly through the length of his body. The amount of bend is controlled by the outside rein and leg. You should be looking ahead between his ears (being aware of the scenery i.e. looking at the trees, helps to prevent you looking down). By keeping the hands evenly placed on either side of his neck, you will be able to keep your horse's head and neck steady. Keeping your inside heel down, ask with your inside calf for the horse to step under his belly with his inside hind leg. Your outside leg behind the girth asks the horse to bend around your inside leg. The reins are used to indicate the position of the forehand as described above. Remember to turn with your horse to keep in balance. Reverse these aids for turning right.

POLE WORK TO HELP AIDS FOR CIRCLES AND TURNS

Turn with your horse when circling, keep your weight down into your inside stirrup and your outside leg behind the girth, and look forward between his ears.

When riding curved lines, it is important to turn in balance with the horse. Set four poles out in a large star shape (see illustration opposite). Begin by riding a large circle around the edge of the poles. Be aware of your horse drifting in or out as you progress around the circle. As you pass the end of each pole, see if your shoulders are parallel to the pole. If you turn your shoulders too far in, your horse will swing his haunches out. This could also indicate that you are trying to turn using too much inside rein and are not allowing the horse to step forward and under with his inside hind leg. If you turn your shoulders to the outside, with your inside shoulder in advance of your outside shoulder, your horse will swing his haunches too far in.

The leg nearest each pole, your inside leg, should be near the girth. Use it to not only keep the horse going, but also to support him as he progresses around the circle. Your outside leg needs to be behind the girth to keep the haunches of your horse following his forehand. Sit on your inside seat bone (nearest the pole) to maintain the flexion through the horse's body. The inside rein controls the amount of flexion to the inside through the horse's head and neck. The outside rein prevents the horse turning his neck more than he should and supports his outside shoulder, stopping him falling out. The angle of your shoulders controls the angle of the horse's shoulders. Turn them the same amount that you want the horse to turn.

Use this star-shaped pole formation to test out the timing of your leg aids with the rhythm of the horse's stride. Try first of all to nudge the horse with your calves as you get to each pole in turn. If he is responsive and going forwards sufficiently, you should not need an aid at every pole. If he is not listening, try an extra leg aid in between the poles as well. Avoid using your legs continually and be aware of how many leg aids you are giving him as you pass through each segment of the circle. This can be quite an eye-opener! By increasing your awareness of the frequency of your actions, you will learn how to become more effective with fewer aids, so that there are spells where you are giving no aids at all, and your horse is continuing of his own volition.

As you get to each pole, check that your turning aids are correct and sufficient. If you drift further away from each one, then your outside aids (rein and leg) need to be firmer. If your horse drifts in then you need more inside leg. You may be leaning in, so rebalance yourself by evening up the weight in your stirrups. You should have a little more weight in your inside stirrup, but too much means that your horse will fall in. Too much weight on the outside

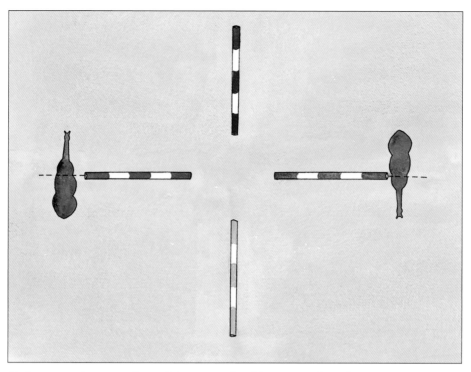

Poles set out in a star shape. Line your shoulders up with each pole in turn to help you to ride an even curve around each quarter of a circle.

stirrup will cause him to fall out. These weight aids can be used judiciously though to make the appropriate corrections in your horse's balance.

The culmination of riding with accurate aids is a balanced horse and rider, both happy in their work. The rider will feel safe and in control and easily able to influence the horse should problems arise.

Transitions

Transitions are vital to teach the horse to engage his hind legs and to lift his back. To ride good transitions, make sure your aids are clear. Prepare each transition by keeping your horse straight and balanced, and ask him to take his weight on his hocks by using half-halts (see page 75) thus ensuring that your horse is softly working into the bridle, i.e. on the bit, so that he benefits from using his back and hindquarters correctly. He should be going forward enough to have impulsion to take him into the next gait, whether you are riding an upward or downward transition, without rushing against your hands. You both need to be in good balance, i.e. you should be able to soften your reins without everything falling to pieces. Check that your own position is good enough for you to have effective use of your legs and upper body, maintaining an elastic contact throughout the exercises.

A straight horse is one whose hind legs follow the tracks of his forelegs. He curves his body by contracting his muscles on the inside, and extending his muscles on the outside. This allows him to move around a circle or a bend. The horse is then described as straight even though he is travelling along a curved line. The horse should remain straight in this way while making transitions on a circle, without any deviation of the haunches either in or out. You need to feel that he is lifting his back underneath you in order for the transition to be clear and precise.

Random Pole Placement for Transition Work

Place your poles in a random manner around your working area. You could spend up to twenty minutes on transition work during your training session but you should not have to go on and on for ages, just long enough to feel an improvement in your horse.

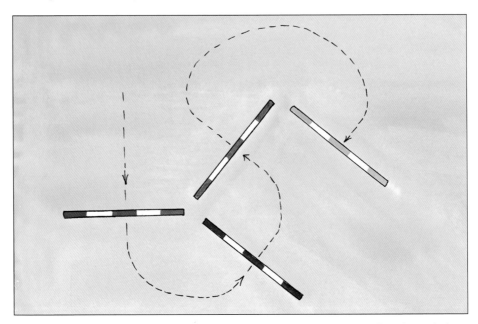

Poles laid out at random. Practise halt transitions in front of each pole and then continue in walk over each one in turn.

Begin in walk, and walk up to each pole in turn. When your horse is right up to the pole with his front feet almost touching it, halt. Reward him by softening your reins a fraction without letting the reins go loose, and then walk on again over the pole, and up to the next one.

Repeat the halt transitions several times until they become precise. By halting right in front of each pole, it gives the horse a barrier to stop by. If your horse is used to walking and trotting over poles and not stopping, you may find he overshoots at first. If this happens, make sure your halt aid is clear enough through your whole body, do not just use the reins to pull. If you pull on the reins, it is likely that he will pull at you and drag you along! Brace your position and stop yourself moving, closing your legs to prevent the horse walking on. As soon as he has responded, remain sitting upright, but remember to cease the leg aid.

Move with him as you ask for an upward transition by allowing the movement of your horse's back muscles to move through your lumbar back and seat bones slightly as he moves forward, then he will not think that you still have the handbrake on. (This does not mean pushing with your seat muscles, but allowing your lower back to swing with the movement of your horse's back muscles). Practise this on both reins and with changes of direction between the poles. From time to time, walk straight over the poles without stopping to make sure that you are maintaining activity.

Proceed to trot. Alternate between rising and sitting trot, to help your horse become more supple through his back. Take your horse around the whole arena (not just around the perimeter) working around the poles to keep you both alert. Begin to trot towards individual poles, make a transition to walk as you get up to them allowing yourself between one and three walk strides before each pole. Walk over each pole and proceed again in trot. This exercise will teach him to listen to you, even if you are asking him to do something different from usual. Because the pole is there, he will engage his hind legs better as he steps over the pole, and because he pushes off his hocks more, you should get an improved transition into trot.

Progress to direct transitions. A direct transition, for example, is from halt to trot, walk to canter etc. and requires good preparation in the form of good half-halts. Try transitions from trot to halt in front of the poles. This again creates much more engagement of the hind legs. Try trotting over the poles and halting afterwards to really make him think. Make transitions in between the random poles as well.

Make a few transitions through trot to canter to prepare him for the pole exercises in canter. Begin by cantering up to an individual pole, and make a transition to trot just before it allowing yourself between one and three trot strides before each one. Trot over the pole, and ask for canter afterwards. This engages his hocks more in the downward transition and thus helps the next upward transition.

Once you have mastered transitions to and from trot and canter in various ways, introduce walk to canter. Alternate trotting to one pole then halting in front of it, then proceeding to walk over it, and then cantering after the pole. Canter to the next, then go over it in canter, making a direct transition from canter to walk afterwards. This is quite an advanced transition to tackle and you will need to build up to this gradually. In this way you can vary the different exercises, making transitions from both walk and trot into canter.

Introduction of Parallel Poles

This can be built up to trotting over three or four parallel poles, (approximately 1.3 m or 4 ft apart) to improve the trot rhythm in between the canter transitions, helping to maintain his outline and cadence (springi-

A good transition from canter to trot approaching trot poles showing the power of the haunches as the horse takes his weight back on his hind legs.

ness). Canter towards the trot poles, giving yourself time to prepare for a smooth downward transition to trot in time for the trot poles.

Once the canter/trot transitions are improved (which could take several weeks!), repeat the exercises introducing canter/walk transitions as mentioned earlier, building up to a sequence of poles in a line at walk distance (approximately 0.8 m or 3 ft). Mix and match the transition work with pole-work sessions for variety, and do not forget to ride normal transitions without the poles to see if they have improved.

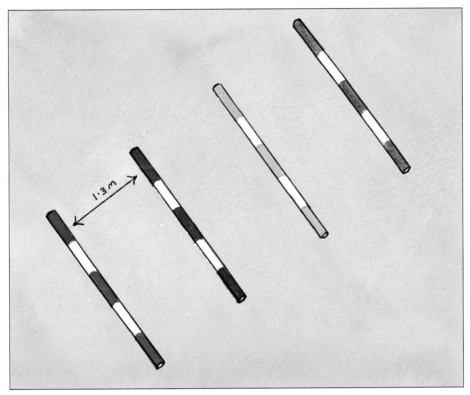

Poles set out for a sequence of trot strides at approximately 1.3 m (4 ft) apart.

Remember to allow your horse to stretch down at regular intervals. Let the reins gradually get longer, encouraging your horse to stretch his neck forward and down to the bit by using your legs and back. Keep your own position upright and balanced so the horse has the confidence to really relax and stretch through his back and neck.

Transition work will strengthen your horse's back muscles and increase the use of his hocks, as he has to bring them more under his body to carry himself.

Straightness

A key objective of any training programme is to develop a supple, athletic horse who can happily carry out the work asked of him and, through proper development, remain free from injury and stress. Straightness is an integral part of this. If your horse is not straight he will not be able to carry himself or you correctly. The long-term result of working a crooked horse can be muscle and ligament misalignment which lead to severe back problems, tendon problems, etc. It is vital that both horse and rider work together to achieve a correct outline and balance.

Riding Straight Between 'Railroad Tracks'

For these exercises, first place four poles like tramlines (see illustration opposite) up the quarter or centre line of your arena. If you have more poles, set out the same formation up both sides of the arena. The poles need to be about 1.3–1.5 m (4–5 ft) apart: make the distance wider for the first few attempts, then narrower as your horse becomes accustomed to going in between the lines of poles.

Remember to change the rein frequently so that your horse does not become one-sided. Most people and horses are stiffer on one side than the other. This will become apparent during this exercise. Sit straight as you ride toward the poles and turn with your horse on the approach. Give yourself enough preparation time by looking at the line you are going to ride and by keeping good body tone in your position to help your horse move with you. As he responds to your turning aids (see page 50), soften the reins a little to allow him to soften through his body and step under more with his back legs. You need to be able to ride straight lines to make sure that your horse is stepping evenly with his legs and that he feels the same on each rein. Once the horse is straight he is easy to manoeuver and his muscles will develop correctly and evenly on both sides of his body.

Turning accurately to the poles takes considerable skill. Remember to turn your horse with your upper body while keeping your legs on his sides to control his hindquarters, preventing them from swinging out as you turn. Bring your horse's forehand into line with your upper body to ensure a good turn. This gives you enough control to carry on in a straight line between

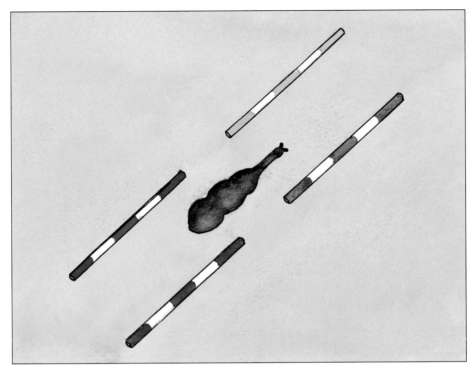

Poles set out as railroad tracks, 1.5 m (5 ft) apart.

the poles. Check your position to ensure that you feel straight in your own body, that you have equal weight in both stirrups and that you are sitting equally on both seat bones.

It helps to split this exercise into three parts: the approach, the straight line and the turn away at the end.

A good turn results in a much more accurate straight line in the centre of the poles. Straighten yourself up after the turn; as a result, your horse will be balanced, straight and correctly on the bit. Straightness guarantees that you are both ready for the next movement. If you lean back instead of turning your shoulders, you will place too much weight on the back of your inside seat bone, causing your horse to bulge outwards and drift away from your seat bone as he turns. You will then find that you will be tempted to be strong on your inside rein to bring him around because he will twist his neck rather than bend through his body, with your planned straight line ending up as a curve! This is one error being compounded by another. Alternatively, if you lean in round the turn, your horse will put more weight on his inside shoulder than his inside hind leg, and his hind legs will drift out. He will then turn on his forehand, rather than his hocks, resulting in a crooked line.

Plan your next turn away from the straight line. Put more weight on your inside stirrup of the new turn without leaning in and turn your shoulders in the new direction. Your outside leg should be behind the girth to start the movement, while your inside leg maintains the forward motion and acts as a 'balancing pole' to support your horse.

Practise walking directly down the middle of the poles. Softly focus your eyes on something in the distance, for example a tree, to keep yourself upright and straight. Try to maintain your straight line before turning away after the poles.

Once you can ride an accurate straight line down the middle of the poles, add in a transition. This could be walk to halt, walk to trot and so on. It is very easy to drift one way or the other, so try to remain straight during your transitions. Alternate the transition work with riding straight through the poles in a good rhythm.

An accurate line ridden between the poles. Both horse and rider are straight and balanced.

WORKING IN TROT AND CANTER

Repeat this exercise in sitting and rising trot, maintaining the straight line. This is excellent practice for competing in dressage, when you usually have small white boards at intervals to keep you in the arena. It is incredibly easy to forget to practise being straight and thus to snake up the long side, a movement which dressage judges tactfully call 'wavering in trot'. You need to be straight in order to progress to varying the walk and trot from collected to medium or extended gaits. These take time to develop and require strength and athleticism from your horse. Work at keeping a good rhythm without slowing down on your approach to the poles.

Before attempting this exercise in canter, ride canter in both directions around the whole school and make sure that your horse is on the bit, responsive to your aids and calm. Other qualities of the canter will improve with this exercise. The poles enable you to easily feel if your horse is swinging his haunches to one side or the other, or if his forehand is pulling you to one side. Make sure you are sitting correctly for whichever canter you have asked for. You should be in the middle of the poles no matter which rein you are on. Because the canter requires positioning the forehand towards the leading leg to keep it balanced, your weight should be on your inside seat bone and your shoulders slightly turned in the direction of the canter, while still travelling in a straight line. Positioning the horse in canter is like riding the merest hint of shoulder-fore, almost imperceptible to the onlooker, but the rider knows that the horse is prepared to turn at the next corner, or to circle, for example. Positioning is about being prepared for the next movement, rather than riding a full-blown shoulder-in. Maintain the canter with your inside leg and keep your horse's haunches in the correct alignment with your outside leg behind the girth. Test the engagement of your horse's inside hind leg by softening your inside rein. It is important to hold your horse's position with your upper body and seat so that you can make fine adjustments with your reins and legs. Vary the canter by collecting the stride for a few steps then extending again, as descibed on page 90.

Circles

To be able to turn your horse in the direction in which you want to go is an essential part of riding. Apart from riding a dressage test where circles are a prerequisite, turns are required in jumping, cross country, hacking etc. The aids for a circle are the basis of the aids for lateral movements. For example, the position of the horse and rider for shoulder-in is the same as for the first step of a circle coming off the track. Travers is the last step of a circle returning to the track. These movements are explained on pages 165 and 169 respectively.

Your ability to keep the bend of your horse's body is essential if you want to keep your circles accurate. On a circle, the inside aids are those to the inside of the bend of the horse and the outside aids are those on the outside of the bend of the horse.

To ride a circle to the right, sit tall in the saddle with your right hip slightly forward, holding the position of your horse's hips with your weight down through your inside (right) seat bone and into your right stirrup to anchor the bend. Your outside (left) leg is placed behind the girth to control the outside of the horse's body. Keeping your hips upright, and not collapsing to the inside, position your shoulders by turning your upper body to the right to correspond with how sharply you want the horse to turn. Keeping your elbows by your sides as you turn prevents you twisting through your waist and helps you to turn your upper body as one unit. This makes your turning aid more clear to the horse and ensures that your horse turns his shoulders to the right with yours.

The inside rein asks your horse to flex his head to the right, while the outside rein controls the amount of bend. It is important to co-ordinate your rein aids. Although they each have a separate job to do, your contact will be uneven if one rein is acting too much, and the other not enough. If your outside rein is too strong, and your inside rein ineffective, your horse will not be able to bend at all in the direction you are going. If your inside rein is too strong and your outside rein loose, your horse will jack-knife with his neck to the inside, but his shoulders will fall away to the outside as they have no support. By keeping one hand on either side of his neck you hold his forehand steady. Look ahead between your horse's ears.

A plastic block makes a good focal point for both horse and rider when riding a circle to help position them correctly.

Keeping your inside heel down, ask with your inside calf for your horse to step under his belly with his inside hind leg. Your legs act in combination to channel the horse into the desired bend, with the outside leg acting to prevent the quarters swinging out. The smaller the circle, the more weight is needed in your right heel and the more both your and your horse's shoulders need to bend to the right. Remember to sit tall to encourage your horse to lift his back, helping him to keep his balance and distributing his weight evenly between his front and back legs. Leaning forward would put your weight over the horse's shoulders, making him carry himself on his forehand. Leaning back would cause him to hollow his back thus rendering him unable to bring his hind legs under his body.

Star-shaped Pole Formation for Circle Work

Set four poles out in an equally spaced star shape. The inner ends of the poles need to be at least 7 m (23 ft) apart, so as to mark a circle with a diameter of about 20 m(65½ ft). This exercise can be made easier by spacing the poles further apart so that a very large circle can be ridden. For a harder exercise, reduce the space between the inner ends.

Begin by walking around the outer edge of the poles to accustom your horse to the circle. Once he starts to relax, spiral in a little so that he is walking over the poles. As your horse picks his feet up over each pole he will round his back to tuck his hindquarters under, so he will want to stretch his neck downwards. Help your horse to do this by softening your hands to encourage him. The poles help because he will want to look down at them. Your horse will pick up an even rhythm in his walk if your poles are evenly spaced. As he becomes more supple, reduce the size of the circle so that he walks over the inner half of the pole. After a few circles, spiral out to make the circle larger again to give him a rest. Once you are happy with the exercise in walk in both directions, proceed to rising trot.

When you have warmed up in trot, aim for the centre of each pole. This will help your horse pick up a rhythmic stride by doing the same number of steps between each pole. Depending upon his length of stride and the precise size of your circle, the horse should consistently take either four or five strides in each segment. Try counting to yourself as you go.

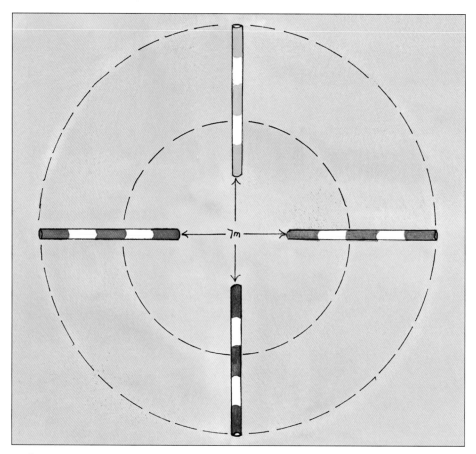

Poles set out in a star shape. A large circle can be ridden around the outside, and a smaller one over the centre of each pole.

Once you have mastered large circles, try individual smaller ones. Each circle will be about 8-10 m (23-33 ft) across. Start by circling around one pole, then add in an extra circle on the other side. Progress to circles around the other two poles, one at a time, until you can do all four in a sequence. As with any new exercise, begin in walk before proceeding to trot, and rise to the trot before moving into sitting trot. Bigger circles are easier, so if you are doing this exercise for the first time, make your star shape really big, so that your smaller circles are about 12 m (39 ft) in diameter. Make sure that you stretch your inside leg down towards each pole and, in sitting trot, that you keep your weight on your inside seat bone.

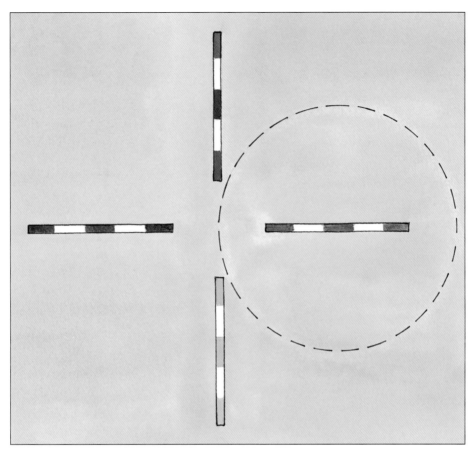

Ride smaller circles of about 8-10 m (26-33 ft) diameter around each individual pole.

Voltes

Once you are happy with your middle-sized circles, come within the inner edges of the poles and ride a small circle of about 6 m (19½ ft) in diameter. This is also known as a volte. This exercise may take some time to achieve correctly. It is most important to remember to really turn your shoulders in alignment with the volte. Keep stretching into your inside stirrup but make sure you do not lean in. Your horse will have to step well under his body with his inside hind leg. If you ride a good volte, you should still be able to soften your inside rein to prove that your horse is correctly bent and balanced.

Pole work is difficult for your horse, so plan regular breaks to give him a stretch. Working large with a long rein around the arena will help him to

A supple horse can do a volte of about 6 m within the inner ends of the poles.

relax and get ready for the next set of exercises. Try circles without the help of the poles when your horse has mastered these exercises – they should be beautifully round and even! It is most important to work equally on both reins with circle work. Even if your horse is stiffer in one direction than the other, he will be helped by this work on alternating reins, rather than going continually around on his bad rein; he needs to work on his good rein to give him the feeling of what he is supposed to be doing!

Stretching

Stretching down is important throughout every aspect of your horse's training. It demonstrates the relaxation and suppleness through a horse's back and hindquarters which requires strength and good balance – otherwise, the horse would topple forward and land on his nose! A novice horse who is not strong and supple through his back and neck will not be able to stretch down as far as a fit, supple and correctly trained grand prix horse. Always test your training by seeing how your horse can stretch. Frequent stretching prevents tension building up and also gives you and your horse valuable thinking and cooling off time in the school. Strong abdominal muscles play a large part in the horse's ability to stretch down. These develop as the horse becomes more adept at working from behind and bringing his hind legs under his body and using these abdominal muscles to do so.

Stretching is important in competition when you need to be able to perform a free walk on a long rein. It also helps to develop the extended gaits, because a horse must reach forward towards the bridle and keep a big arch in his neck in order to extend his stride. If a horse stretches his leg out in front, he will put it on the ground under his nose but not in front of it, thus stressing the importance of developing a long, arched neck.

Outline

A good outline is one where the horse appears to be rounded evenly over the top line of his body. The horse should resemble a bridge, with his back lifted and with his legs being the bridge supports.

A horse with a good outline has strong, defined muscles; free-moving gaits and is happy in his work. The outline develops in stages throughout a horse's training, with a good outline indicative of correct work. There is no short cut to achieving this; it takes time, understanding and close observation of the way in which a horse is developing. A poor outline affects the horse's movement, attitude, physique and wellbeing. Long-term problems can stem from a poor outline. Torn muscle becomes weak and ineffective and can result in unbalanced movement. If the ligaments, which support the joints, are over-stretched, the joints lose stability and can become strained through excess movement. Tendons, which attach muscle to bone, become strained and damaged if the muscles are weak and under-developed. The alternative is a horse who resembles a peacock with a fast, flat stride and the 'bridge' sunk in the middle.

The horse should appear to have a bridge-like construction when working correctly and lifting his back.

NOVICE (TRAINING LEVEL) HORSE

A novice horse will have an outline like a low, arched bridge. He should appear to be evenly arched from his nose to his tail, with enough weight taken on his hind end to avoid looking as if he is going downhill. If he does, he is on his forehand and will feel heavy on the reins. A novice horse needs to develop correctly in his working gaits, whereby a more or less even loading of all four limbs is established. This does not mean taking a short contact to restrict the front end; instead, it is the ability to take weight on his haunches. This is the true meaning of collection.

ELEMENTARY (FIRST LEVEL) HORSE

A horse working at elementary level will have developed more strength through his body and should be able to carry himself in a slightly more arched bridge, with his neck lifted more from the withers than the novice horse. This is relative elevation, rooted in some lowering of the haunches. The middle section of his body should appear to be higher, with his stomach muscles working to keep his back up and his hind legs more under his body. You only need enough collection to perform the required movements, so it is a mistake to force a horse's outline into a more compressed shape than needed at any stage. The result of this will be a tense horse with restricted gaits. An elementary horse's gaits should be big and free but without him thundering around at speed!

MEDIUM/ADVANCED MEDIUM (SECOND OR THIRD LEVEL) HORSE

A medium/advanced medium level horse should look rounded through his body. His neck carriage should be a higher arch than the elementary horse as a result of better mobility through his back allied with stronger haunches, giving more carrying power to his hind legs and a greater ability to collect. If the collection is correct, then the extended gaits will flow forward without excessive driving aids from the rider – a bit like a speedboat zooming off once it has enough revs from the engine! Cadence, or springiness, should be apparent in his strides, with his back swinging in a supple way which enables the rider to sit still and be carried by the horse, rather than bounced all over the place.

ADVANCED (FOURTH LEVEL) HORSE

The advanced horse should look like a steep bridge lifted up at the front end. He should still have a rounded appearance through his body, but his poll will be higher, with a steeply arched neck as a consequence of his hindquarters being tucked under. This horse should look as if he could sit on the ground without much effort and display a greater degree of flexion in his leg joints, giving more spring or cadence to his gaits than horses at an earlier stage of training. There should be a measured, powerful look about the advanced horse's gaits and he should look confident and sure about his balance and rhythm. Both horse and rider should look elegant and appear to work without really working. It comes back to a good performance appearing effortless – although if it actually were, we would all be covered in rosettes!

It is important to take time at the outset of your horse's training programme to allow him to develop correct musculature, resulting in a correct outline, which is the vital building block to training up to advanced level. Without the correct basic work, faults will occur at later stages, with the only solution being going back to basics, whatever your horse's level of work, and re-establishing his ability to stretch down via correct contact with the bit.

Lungeing over Poles

Pole work can be extremely valuable for a horse who is tense through his back and does not work in a relaxed manner. It acts as a distraction from his problems by giving him something else to concentrate on, provided that it is carried out constructively, with correct distances, heights, exercises etc.

To begin, warm up on the lunge, then attach a chambon to make sure that he is as supple and relaxed through his back as you can get him. Detach the chambon and then lunge him over a single pole on the ground in walk, keeping the circle big enough so that he can approach the pole straight on. Repeat this until he is happy and relaxed. If your horse is very tense he might jog over the pole; if this happens, use your voice and half-halts on the lunge line to help him understand that you want him to walk. Remember to praise your horse as soon as he does it correctly. You need to wait for your horse to walk over the pole and stretch his neck down to show that he is using his back correctly. Poles have the advantage of making him pick his feet up and engaging his hocks and shoulders. Be very patient with a tense horse, but confident and in control of your actions, so that he does not receive any mixed messages from you. He must know when he is good, and when he has misunderstood you.

Try this exercise first without the chambon but you might need to revert to it again if your horse hollows his back and raises his head. If the exercise

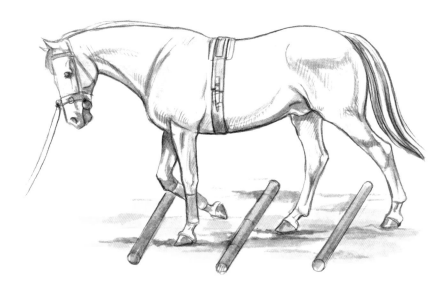

Lungeing the horse in walk over a sequence of poles, encouraging him to stretch through his back and neck.

goes well, walk him over the same pole in long, low side reins to encourage him to use his back and work into a contact at the same time. Be careful not to have the side reins too short at this stage; if you take your time to prepare him and are very observant of his reactions, he should accept the side reins easily. This might sound painstaking, but it is worth taking time in the beginning, otherwise the tension will keep reappearing.

Progress to walking over three or four poles placed about 0.8 m apart, which is the distance for an average walk stride (a step). As the horse might be tempted to jump two poles, always progress from one to three. If he has a naturally good outline you will be able to do this exercise without side reins, but if he needs guidance to help him carry himself and remain in a good outline at this stage of training, use either a chambon or side reins. Correctly used, either will help your horse to work into a steady contact with a swinging back and active hind legs.

Once you are happy with the exercise in walk, follow exactly the same process in a steady trot. Place the poles wider apart: 1.3 m is an average trot stride. Keep it steady at the beginning – if your horse goes too fast, he will become tense and unsure again. It might take several sessions to reach this stage. Patience is the key to relaxing a tense horse: unless he is relaxed with this unridden exercise, he will not use his back properly under saddle.

Finish each session with your horse walking and/or trotting over the same poles in a natural stretch down, without the chambon or side reins, so that he finishes feeling unrestricted, free, relaxed and ready for your next session!

Walking Over Parallel Poles

Begin with parallel poles in a sequence spaced for walk at 0.8 m approximately depending on the length of your horse's stride. Four should be enough for this exercise but you can progress to six or eight if your horse becomes very supple. Walk over the line of poles with long reins, so that you can just keep a very light contact on the bit to guide him, and notice how your horse holds his neck naturally. Does he stretch his neck out straight in front, or does he hold his neck to one side? Also does he walk in a straight line or not?

If your horse is not straight, make sure first of all that you are sitting straight in the saddle with your stirrups level and that the saddle is not over to one side. Make sure that the contact in your hands is even, keeping your hands level. Take up a contact, with the reins as long as possible. If your horse is willing to stretch straight away, you will have a longer rein than if your horse is reluctant to stretch.

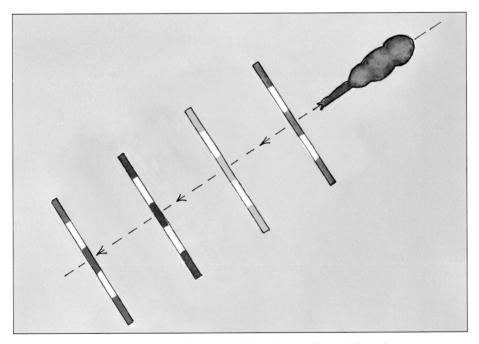

A sequence of poles can either be set at 0.8 m for walk, or 1.3 m for trot.

You may have recently acquired a new horse with upside-down musculature. He would have a very developed underside to his neck and a top line like the spout of a tea pot, with little or no muscle in front of his withers, and over-developed muscle at the top end of his neck. This horse would be extremely reluctant to stretch, owing to his muscles being incorrectly developed. There may be underlying problems causing tension through the shoulders and neck. These things need investigating if they are suspected.

Use your lower legs to encourage the horse to walk forward into the contact. If he does not want to stretch, you will need a firmer, more supportive upper body and arm position to show him what to do and maintain his head and neck position, while you encourage him forward with your lower leg. As he accepts the bit, he should begin to reach down for the contact. When he does, soften your arms and back muscles in order to move with him, without going too slack and losing support altogether in your upper body. Keep tone in your stomach muscles to keep everything under control!

As he steps over the poles, he is encouraged to use his hind legs with more flexibility, beginning to use his back muscles, and to want to stretch his neck downwards. He should also want to look down at the poles to see where he is putting his feet. Try to stay sitting upright in the saddle, to avoid putting the horse's weight over his forehand. It is hard work for him to pick up his feet and stretch his neck at the same time, but just keep reminding him to keep moving with squeezes from your lower legs alternately in time with the walk. You may need to tap him with a schooling whip on his back leg to help. As he stretches down, ease the reins forward by extending your arms forward. If you just let the reins go, he will lose the stretch and poke his nose forward instead.

Relaxation and harmony between horse and rider. The contact remains elastic as the horse confidently stretches into long reins.

Using poles in the star pattern, as well as in a line, will also encourage the horse to look where he is putting his feet, thus lowering his head and neck and stretching through his back. The poles help the horse to be more athletic through his body, more flexible through his joints, and to develop the swinging motion of his back that is so important when carrying the rider in balance.

Stretching at the Rising Trot

Many riders ignore rising trot, because they do not understand how useful it is in any horse's training programme. Rising trot can encourage a reluctant horse to go forward or persuade a forward-going horse to slow down. It can influence the momentum of the trot, affects the way in which a horse uses his back and, consequently, how he stretches. Frequently changing diagonals (and direction) enables you to feel if your horse takes strides of unequal length; this work encourages him to use both hind legs evenly in diagonal pairs. Maintain the stretched outline by keeping your position and balance correct. Your upper body should remain upright or very slightly in front of the vertical. Any backward tendencies mean that you will be left behind the movement of the trot. Because the horse is moving forward, you need to be rising forward, otherwise the horse will move ahead of you and you will return to the saddle with a thump as you are left behind!

If you can do this well, then try to keep the stretch while you are in a light forward seat, keeping your seat out of the saddle. This encourages even more use of the horse's back. If you can keep this position over the poles, you will feel your horse's stride become springier underneath you.

Start by trotting over a single pole, then progress to four poles on the ground, set at about 1.3 m (4 ft) apart. A more advanced exercise is to try first one raised pole, then a line of four poles raised on blocks at the lowest height or four cavalletti set at their lowest height, keeping the stretched outline through your horse. This will really strengthen the horse's back and neck muscles. You have to have good balance for this, as the horse will pick his feet up even more. About three times in each direction will be enough to start with as it is quite strenuous exercise. Build up gradually to riding this exercise for fifteen minutes twice a week to build up the strength in his joints.

Stretching on a Circle

Lay the poles out in the star pattern on a 20 m circle and ride the same stretch, first of all in walk, then in rising trot. If all goes well, then do it in a light seat. This is quite difficult, as you have to remember to turn your body as well. Your horse may have more difficulty stretching and bending in one direction than the other. This is a sign of a physical problem (either his or yours!) even if it is simply uneven muscle development. If he is struggling, check you own position first; make sure that you have enough weight on your inside stirrup, have turned your upper body as one unit and have not left your elbows doing their own thing.

In between circling over the poles and stretching, go around the whole arena keeping the stretch. This should give the horse confidence to move around the school in a big, elastic stride, in balance and not relying on your reins for support. If, however, he has a problem then you need to help him. If he rushes off, you need to half-halt several times to rebalance him on his hind legs and re-establish 'four-wheel drive'; returning to the poles will help. If he becomes crooked, return to the first set of poles to even him up again and to check his straightness.

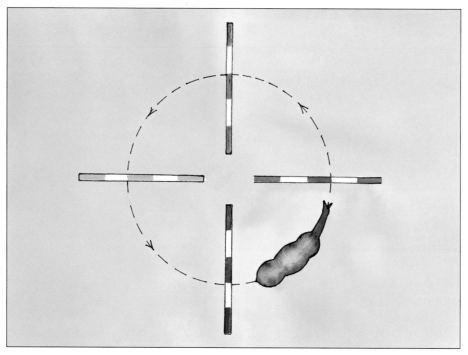

Poles in a star pattern encourage more activity of the hind legs and back muscles during stretching.

Half-halts and Quarter Pirouettes

Half-halts

The definition of a half-halt in the FEI dressage rulebook is:

> The half-halt is hardly visible, almost simultaneous, co-ordinated action of the seat, the leg and the hand of the rider, with the object of increasing the attention and balance of the horse before the execution of several movements or transitions to lesser or higher paces. In shifting slightly more weight onto the horse's quarters, the engagement of the hind legs and the balance on the haunches are facilitated, for the benefit of the lightness of the forehand and the horse's balance as a whole.

In essence, the half-halt is a quick correction to your horse's balance and obedience which encourages him to take more weight on his hind legs in order to lighten his forehand. However, in order to adjust your horse's balance and to half-halt correctly you need to establish your own balance in the correct riding position first.

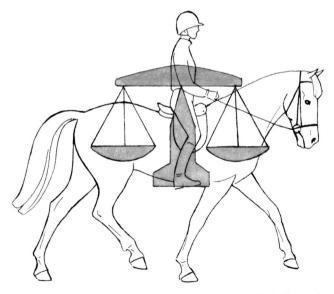

Visualize yourself and your horse as a pair of perfectly balanced scales.

Think of a pair of scales. If your horse is nicely balanced, you are the balancing pole in the middle. Your hands are light, your horse is supple and springy and your position feels natural. Your aids will be minimal and your body tone subtle, with just enough tension to enable you to keep your position. If this is not an accurate picture of your riding, you and your horse need to learn the half-halt.

The half-halt is your body saying 'listen' to your horse. For instance, if he is leaning against your hands, say 'no' by becoming braced or solid in your trunk, firming your tummy and lower back and closing your lower thigh, knees and calves against the saddle. Your reins, but predominantly the outside one, need to become firmer, matching the tone of your lower leg. Your horse should respond to your half-halt, or 'no' feeling, by hesitating momentarily. As soon as you feel this hesitation you must immediately soften your legs, waist and outside rein again, encouraging your horse to move forwards. All of this happens within one step! As a response to your half-halt, he will lift under the saddle, feeling as though he is humping his lumbar back under you. Your response must be to soften the reins slightly, not so that they become loose, just softer, like elastic – first the inside, then the outside – to prevent him leaning against the reins and to reward him for taking his weight back on his hind legs. As the horse takes the weight back on his hind legs, you should feel the reins soften slightly as he becomes less reliant on them. His neck should remain arched evenly along its length. (This is not to be confused with the horse coming behind the bit and shortening his neck; his neck would appear tight and wrinkly just in front of the withers if this were the case.) This is the moment when you soften a little as well. Your horse learns to balance himself with a much lighter contact on the reins when you ease them without dropping the contact. This is like saying, 'Step under my seat and get off my reins!'

Do not make the common mistake of tightening your buttock muscles which will squeeze you out of the saddle. Your bottom should remain soft, helping you to remain upright on your seat bones. Your position in the saddle must not alter visibly: only the *tone* of your body changes. Use as many half-halts as you need until you feel your horse become soft in your hands, round in his back and mentally receptive. Bear in mind that you might need several half-halts in quick succession to prepare for a transition.

STAR-SHAPED POLE FORMATION FOR HALF-HALTS

Set your poles out in the star pattern and ride a big circle around them. Halt as you get to the end of each pole, then alternate the halt with a half-halt at each pole. To ensure that you remain upright, line your shoulders up with each pole. Progress to half-halting at each pole. If you lose the feeling of the half-halt, return to the halt transitions.

Quarter Pirouettes

A quarter pirouette is a turn around the hocks performed in walk or canter. In walk, the hind legs walk part of a small circle, as though stepping around a dinner plate on the ground. The front legs take bigger sideways steps and cross over. Two or three steps are all that is required for a quarter pirouette. Their execution teaches the horse to move away from your outside leg, which is useful for turning and for half pass, for example. Quarter pirouettes should be developed from the half-halt; to be properly executed, they need a light forehand. To ask for a quarter pirouette, sit on your inside seat bone and, maintaining an upright position, turn your upper body in the direction of the pirouette. Unless you turn with the horse, he will not understand what you want. Your outside leg is more dominant but your inside leg maintains the necessary rhythm. If you have good energy in the gait, your inside leg aid will be quite small. The inside leg must stay long with your heel down to hold the turn on the spot and to prevent the pirouette becoming a normal turn (quarter circle). Keep your elbows by your sides and avoid pulling him around with your inside rein, because this will cause him to swing his haunches out. Keep a firm outside rein to prevent forward motion and, turning your upper body, move your horse's forehand around. Keep your inside rein soft as you turn.

SQUARE-SHAPED POLE FORMATION FOR QUARTER PIROUETTES

Set the poles out in a square. Go beyond the end of each pole to turn. As your horse's hind legs reach the end of each pole and you have half-halted, make the four corner points quarter pirouettes. Your horse must keep the rhythm of his walk as you turn. His hind legs take small steps as he turns around each corner of the square. His front legs should take big steps sideways, crossing over as you go. Just take two or three steps to line your horse up with the next pole. Ride a straight line directly to the end and repeat the exercise. Once he has turned, sit straight again and use your inside leg to send your horse straight on.

By using four plastic cones to make a square you can then progress to riding half pirouettes around them quite easily. Make sure that you always ride your horse straight forward after each turn to check that you are both balanced. At a later stage, this exercise can be useful for developing canter pirouettes, beginning with quarter pirouettes around the square of poles, then around cones to progress to half pirouettes.

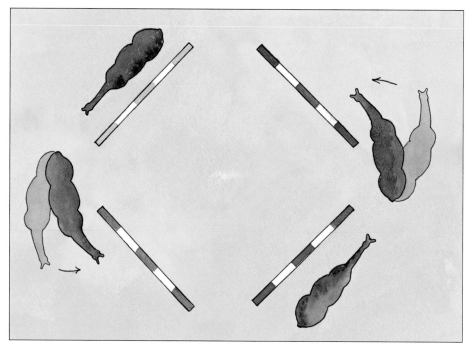

Poles set out in a square. Ride a quarter pirouette at each corner of the square.

A well-executed quarter pirouette, showing the lightness of the forehand and a soft inside rein. Both horse and rider are turning together, though the rider's inside heel is slightly raised.

Corners, Shallow Loops and Serpentines

Being able to change direction and to turn has many applications. Turning easily means that you have great control over your horse and are therefore safer, not only in the school, but also out hacking, riding across country or jumping. Serpentines are terrific flexibility exercises and should be an integral part of your training.

Corners

Set the four poles out in a square that is large enough to allow you to ride around the outside of them in a big square. This is useful if your horse tends to fall in around corners. If your horse tends to drift his haunches to the outside, set the poles in a larger square and ride around the inside of the poles to help you to keep his haunches under control.

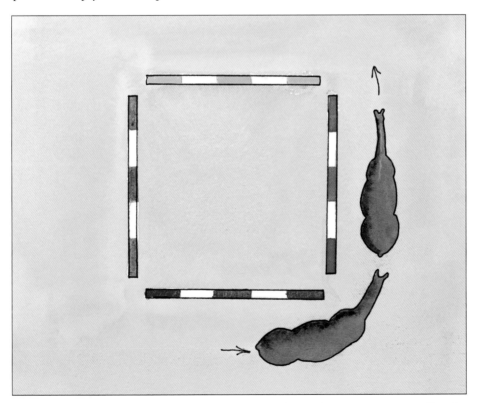

Poles marking out a square to improve the riding of accurate corners. Set the poles in a larger square to ride corners on the inside of the poles.

Begin the exercise by riding a square around the four poles and ride each corner as a simple quarter turn, i.e. a quarter volte. Count the number of steps that you take for each one – they should be the same! If your horse's walk is more collected, you will need up to six steps; four will probably be enough in a medium walk. The same principle applies when you try this exercise in trot or canter.

Keep the sides of your square straight by using the poles as a guide. Sit up in a good position while maintaininng slight flexion to the inside through your horse so that you are ready for each corner. To ride the quarter circles, use your inside leg to keep the turn clear and prevent the horse falling in (avoid leaning in yourself). You need to support the horse on the outside rein, but also allow him to turn around the corner, as the horse steps correctly under with his inside hind leg to propel himself around the turn. Your inside rein should be soft as your shoulders turn with your horse. When you complete each turn, ride your horse straight alongside the pole, still retaining the flexion through his body to the inside. This is preparation for the next turn that you come to and applies whether you are riding around the inside or the outside of the square.

Shallow loops

Set the poles out in two parallel lines and stagger them, leaving large gaps in between. Space them out so that you can ride a slalom from one pole to the next.

The loops should be even curves – part of a circle. These loops are joined together by a short straight line that occurs as you cross the centre line each time. These few steps give you the opportunity to straighten your horse after each turn and to prepare him for the next. This must be done smoothly, otherwise you will unbalance him. Maintain the bend through your horse's body as you ride each loop, then half-halt, positioning yourself and your horse for the next turn, then ride forward into the turn in a good rhythm. The loops should flow together easily. Concentrate on feeling if your horse's hind legs are following his forehand, or if they are drifting out on the turns. Ride accurately towards the centre of each pole, aiming your outside knee at it. If you maintain the correct bend of your horse, he should be bending away from the pole as his belly gets to it. A common mistake is to use too much inside rein to bring the horse's head around; if you do this, you will feel your horse's shoulders fall out towards

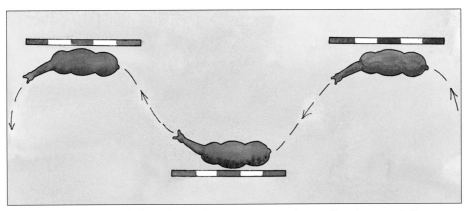

Staggered poles to aid the riding of accurate, even loops. Set them at 6-8 m (19¹/₂-26 ft) apart.

the pole. Your outside leg will prevent this happening provided you are not using your inside rein too much. Make sure that you turn your shoulders with your horse and keep your inside leg on to keep him stepping into your outside rein.

Riding shallow loops. Prepare for the new bend as you pass from one pole to the next.

Serpentines

Once you are happy with shallow loops, progress to a serpentine. Set the poles in a line down the centre line of the school so that you can ride over each in turn. You can put in as many loops as you like. Using fewer, big loops, three for example, is easier than four or five smaller ones. With a four-loop serpentine you will be coming across the centre line three times and will need three poles equally spaced. A three-loop serpentine requires two straight lines across the centre. Aim to ride directly at the middle of each pole across the middle of the school.

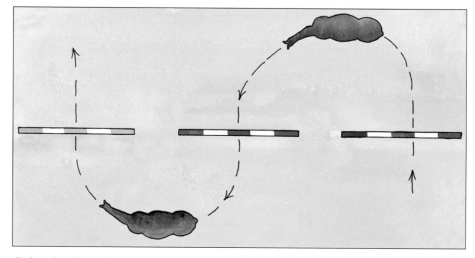

Poles placed up the centre line. Aim at riding accurately over the centre of each pole.

Ride large loops touching the sides of the arena and, to keep a regular bend throughout the loop, think of them as a section of a circle. Straighten yourself and your horse by sitting exactly level as you come in line with the next pole. If you aim straight, he will take an elevated step over the pole to aid the engagement of his hind legs. Maintain your horse's outline by keeping an elastic contact. If your horse rounds his back really well as this exercise progresses, remember to reward him with a softer contact (do not just drop the contact, or he will fall on his forehand). Immediately after the pole, prepare your horse for the next loop in the other direction. Make sure he is flexing through his whole body and not just turning his head. Remember that the action of your outside leg helps to bring him around your inside leg and that this should help with your horse's balance. When you reach the point where you want to turn into the loop, turn your upper body toward the direction in which you want to go.

Gaits: Improving Rhythm

Rhythm is one of the most fundamental qualities of a good gait, whether it is walk, trot or canter. Incorrect riding can easily spoil it, and a regular beat can become choppy, irregular steps. Developing a good sense of rhythm is easier for people who have an aptitude for music or dancing, but transferring that sense of rhythm to riding a horse can be difficult, rather like dancing with a partner with two left feet (it is usually the rider who has the two left feet!).

Set the poles out in a star shape with a 10 m (33 ft) gap between the inner edges so that you can ride a circle within them. You need enough space on the outside to ride around them on a very large circle. If you are attempting this exercise for the first time, and you are not sure how supple your horse is, put a 12 m (39 ft) gap between the inner edges.

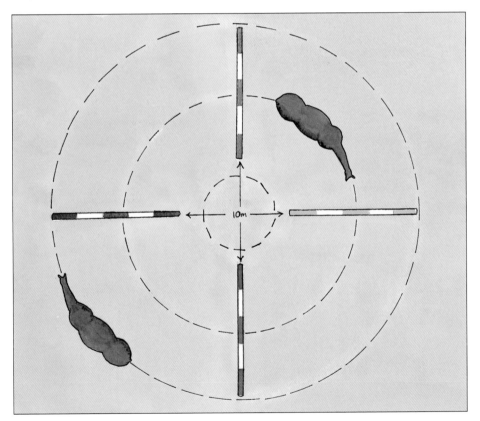

Poles set out in a star-shape. Circles of different sizes are indicated. Allow room for a 10 m circle in the middle. Count the number of strides between the poles to establish a rhythm.

Walk

Begin by stretching your horse down around the school to establish relaxation through his back making sure he is loosened up and supple. Using half-halts, encourage him to lift his back and take up the contact so that he is correctly on the bit, with his nose vertical to the ground. Establishing medium walk, decrease the size of the circle gradually until you are riding a small circle within the centre of the ends of the poles. You will need to keep a really correct bend through your horse's body to match the size of the circle you are riding; he will need to bend more through his body on the smaller one. While you are spiralling in, count your horse's steps in a regular rhythm. The speed of the steps should remain the same on the small circle as they did on the bigger one. His outline should remain the

Maintaining bend and rhythm while spiralling in to a smaller circle.

same throughout. Decrease the circle very gradually. If your horse has a problem at any time, return to the larger circle to regain his confidence.

During this exercise start with a long rein on the big circle, taking up the contact as you spiral in. Increase the amount of bend through his body on the small circle. As the circle grows smaller, maintain an elastic contact without restricting his back movement. This helps the horse to use his back muscles correctly and become suppler through his joints.

Maintain your horse's outline and balance in the walk with frequent discreet half-halts so as not to disturb the rhythm as you decrease the size of the circle. Keep yourself in a good, upright position with your weight into your inside stirrup, without leaning in. You should feel the horse engage his hocks and begin to pick up his feet. He will feel as though he has lifted his back underneath the saddle. As you circle around the poles on the big circle, count the steps. You should pass the end of each pole with the same number of steps in between, e.g. seven steps to the end of each one. As you spiral inwards there should be fewer steps between each pole but they should still be evenly matched.

Begin to spiral out on to a larger circle again, passing over the poles at first, and ending up on a large circle around the outside of the poles. As you go back out, keep the impulsion with your inside leg so that he does not drop behind the vertical and lose the length of his stride or the rhythm. Repeat the exercise again, this time keeping him in a more collected walk, with a raised neck, the poll being the highest point.

Extend the stride and encourage him to lower and stretch his neck so he is really striding out in walk and still working through his back. Lengthening the stride is discussed on page 88. You should still be counting the steps.

Trot

Try the same exercise in trot. Count the number of strides between each pole as you pass by on the outside. Begin in rising trot and as you begin spiralling in over the poles, make sure you can feel the horse's back rounding up underneath you. As you get to the small circle in the centre, take sitting trot to really get the feel of using your inside seat bone to maintain the bend and balance. The rhythm should remain the same as you circle. Begin to spiral out and take rising trot. Keep your body in the same tempo in the rising trot all the time. Keep the horse in a stretched, round outline to encourage the swing of his back. When you are outside the poles again, develop the trot into a bigger stride. The rhythm of your rising must stay the same. In this way you can prevent the horse from speeding up. Stretch his neck more down while he is in a bigger stride to really increase the suppleness through his back. Aim to ride the same stretched outline on the smaller circle in the center of the poles, as you do around the outside of the poles on the large circle. You should end up with a powerful steady supple trot, being able to keep the outline and the rhythm of the gait after this exercise.

Make sure that you maintain the bend of the circle throughout and that your horse has a great amount of impulsion coming from his hindquarters. His inside hind leg should reach well under his body and his shoulders should be free and allowing a good long stride. The important thing is to keep counting the same rhythm outside the poles as you had using the poles, and not to speed up.

Canter

This exercise also works well in the canter. Establish a good quality, working canter around the school by making frequent transitions between trot and canter and, once your horse is supple enough, walk to canter, to make sure that he has his hocks under him. You may need to take yourself off around the school at regular intervals as a mental break and a stretch. Avoid trying to turn the horse with your inside rein, as this will unbalance him and cause his hind legs to swing out, so you will lose the engagement of his hocks, and you will end up holding him up with your inside rein as he will lean on it if given the option. Take care to turn your shoulders around the circle with the horse.

After these exercises, ride around the school in each gait. Practise stretching him down, then asking him to work in a rounder outline through his back again. The rhythm should not alter.

Collection and Extension

Collection

Collecting aids are used for correcting the balance of the horse. Before the horse can lengthen his stride, he needs to be able to collect and take his weight on his hocks in order to propel himself forward with elevation in the gait. Without being able to collect, the horse would just run faster and faster, losing rhythm and balance. When collecting the horse, it is important to avoid loss of impulsion or power. Collecting is vastly more than just a shortening of the horse's stride; it is a lift of his back and a lowering of his hindquarters as he takes more of his weight behind. Half-halts collect your horse; if he is collecting correctly from your seat and leg aids, your hands should be able to maintain a light, elastic contact with your horse's mouth. These principles apply to walk, trot and canter.

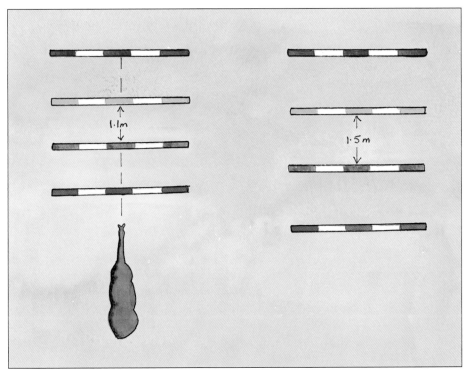

Poles set out at approximately 1.1 m (3½ ft) for collected trot, and 1.5 m (5 ft) for extended trot. They would need to be approximately 0.6 m (2 ft) for collected walk and 1 m (3 ft) for extended walk.

POLE WORK FOR COLLECTED WALK AND TROT

By using parallel poles to work over at a close distance, the horse has to take more elevated steps. More of his energy is converted into lifting his feet up, rather than striding forward. The inclusion of quarter and half pirouettes in walk to aid collection is useful. After completing your quarter pirouette, move briskly forward in a straight line. Use this exercise to prepare your horse for the half pirouette. Maintain a fairly upright position to help balance the horse, and prevent him tipping you forward onto his forehand, as this would completely destroy the exercise. Combining the poles with a half pirouette at each end is a really good exercise to develop collection.

Position a half pirouette to the left so that you are three or four walk steps away from the line of poles on its completion, then proceed directly over the poles in walk to use the propulsion from the hocks that you have just generated. After the poles, continue for another three or four steps, and prepare for another half pirouette to the right to come back over the poles in the other direction. Move off in walk over the poles. Once you have mastered this exercise in walk, progress to going directly into trot from the half pirouettes, making sure that you straighten yourself and your horse first. Make your transitions into and out of collected trot three or four strides away from the poles so that you have time to straighten your horse before the poles.

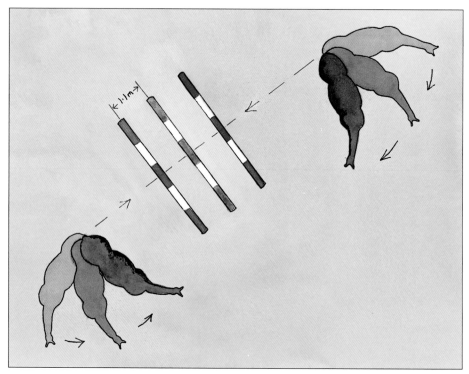

Poles set for collected trot showing half pirouettes at either end.

Extension

Lengthening the stride encourages forward motion in the horse. Before riding the horse forward into more extended strides, an element of collection is needed to maintain the lightness of the forehand and to prevent him running against the reins, and he should have enough weight on his hocks to be able to increase the length and power of his stride without losing balance. Extension is more to do with allowing the horse to propel himself forward in walk, trot or canter, rather that having to shove him along.

POLE AND CAVALLETTI WORK FOR EXTENDED WALK AND TROT

By setting the poles parallel to each other, about 1.5 m (5 ft) apart for extended trot or 1 m apart for extended walk, your horse will have to really push off his hocks to reach for the longer stride that he has to take. Make sure that you keep in balance and do not get left behind. Gradually increase the distance between the poles by 0.2 m (½ ft) at a time as he becomes stronger physically. This may take several months of work, gradually improving the length of stride. Maintain an elastic contact with the reins, so as not to restrict the shoulder movement. Your horse will need the support of the reins though to give him the confidence to reach forward with his front legs. He has to lengthen his frame in order to lengthen his stride. His neck needs to stretch forward and his nose should be allowed to be just in front of the vertical to achieve the free, forward movement required.

Extended trot developing over cavalletti to maintain elevation in the steps, thus keeping a big, free stride. The cavalletti are set low, to avoid asking too much of the horse and perhaps inducing tension in the back.

When riding extended walk over poles or cavalletti, it is important to be supple in your lower back and hip joints to allow as much freedom of movement in the horses's back as possible. Maintain an elastic contact with the bit to allow your horse to reach forward into the bridle

When extending the trot over poles or cavalletti, you need to keep a balanced, rising trot to enable you to follow the propulsion of the stride without being left behind. This position enables you to use your lower back to amplify the swing of the trot. The horse should not speed up his rhythm but take bigger and more powerful strides. His extended gaits should remain soft to sit to if he is using his back correctly with his weight carried mainly on his hind legs. It is important not to actually lean back against the reins as this would cause too strong a rein contact. Your lower legs give driving aids to the horse to tell him to move forward. Your thighs maintain his and your balance by keeping contact with the saddle; they should not grip, but are needed to maintain stability. It is important to remember not to push the horse along with your seat muscles because the seat bones then tend to dig into the saddle, not allowing the horse to maintain the roundness of his back as he moves forward. This will result in the horse hollowing his back and running forward with his nose too high. The lumbar spine is the driving force. Your heels must remain down to maintain calf stretch, with the ankles acting as shock absorbers. He should feel as though he is bounding forwards with the power of a speedboat!

COLLECTION AND EXTENSION IN CANTER

Collection and extension in canter is best ridden between two poles, or a pole and a fence, to help keep the horse straight (see page 61). Place the poles so that you have plenty of space at both ends to ride away on a large curve and back again to the poles. Establish a working canter around your schooling area, and then ride straight between the poles, collecting the stride as you get there with half-halts (see page 75). Maintain this collection for a few strides, then allow your horse to go forward in working canter again in the direction of the canter lead, i.e. ride away to the left if you are in left canter, and to the right if you are in right lead canter. This may sound obvious, but if you cannot tell which canter lead you are on at all times, you will have a problem! Once you have established changes within the gait from collected canter to working canter, try extending the canter stride as you ride away from the poles. This exercise can also be used to establish transitions betwen collected, working and extended trot, and collected, medium and extended walk.

Rein-back

Asking your horse to go backwards is extremely useful at times, for, for example, opening gates, avoiding pot-holes etc. apart from being a disciplined movement requiring a supple back and responsiveness to your seat. It is also a useful exercise in the context of increasing engagement of the hocks in collection. When correctly executed, the rein-back involves the horse stepping backwards in diagonal pairs in a regular two-time rhythm. He should pick his feet up clearly and not scuff his toes along the ground.

Moving Straight

One of the biggest problems encountered when riding rein-back is keeping your horse absolutely straight; many horses swing their haunches one way or the other while the rider steers with the reins. Unfortunately, it only makes matters worse when your horse's front end sways from side to side. Snaking backwards like this also causes your horse to lose control over his haunches and straightness. Any significant one-sidedness should be remedied before starting rein-back. An overtly crooked horse is bound to rein-back crooked.

To begin these exercises, set out a corridor of poles to guide you. They need to be about 1.5 m (5 ft) apart. Place them either up the long side of the arena, so that you also have the fence to help you keep straight, or on the centre line. The latter is a better option if you have a horse who likes to squash you against the fence or who has a tendency to lean towards it.

Rounding the Back

Once your horse has warmed up, work on transitions between trot and walk, then trot and halt. This helps to lift his back and to ask for a degree of collection in his gaits, depending on his stage of training; a more advanced horse will be able to collect more easily. Make sure that you can feel your horse's back coming up underneath the saddle. His neck will soften into a round outline and the contact will feel elastic. Riding rein-back correctly improves the engagement of his hind legs and teaches him to tuck his haunches further under, so that it looks as though his back end is lower

Rein-back ridden between a corridor of poles helps to keep the horse straight.

than his front. As your horse steps backwards, his neck outline should remain the same, but this is only possible if his hind legs are lined up with his front legs. It is rather like reversing a trailer: you need to maintain the feeling that the vehicle is directly in front of the trailer to push it back straight. If you overdo the steering, you end up with the trailer swinging round to one side.

Preparation is important. Your horse needs to understand *how* to round his back in order to rein-back. Otherwise, if a rider pulls the horse back with the reins, he will throw his nose up and hollow his back, tensing his neck muscles. Inevitably, this results in the horse shooting backwards (or sideways) with his head up, which is not comfortable for either the horse or the rider. The horse is then unable to reverse in a straight line because he cannot bring his hind legs underneath him and is left swinging his haunches from side to side and waddling in a crab-like fashion.

Rider's Position

To ride a correct rein-back, you need to halt square with good balance – in other words, your horse should not lean on your hands for support. Make sure that you ask for the halt correctly by sitting up straight and halting your horse with your back and stomach muscles, with the weight in your legs down in your stirrups. Close your lower legs enough to ask your horse's hind legs to come under his body, encouraging his back to lift up under the saddle. You should feel as though you are sitting on a slight hump, rather than in a hollow. To ask your horse to go backwards, ease your weight slightly towards your crotch, so that you feel as though you are sitting closer to the pommel of the saddle. Stretch your thighs down and back so that both of your feet are slightly behind the girth. Ease your shoulders a few centimetres forward so that you feel as though your weight is forward over your knees. This adjustment of movement is miniscule; you do not need to throw yourself over your horse's withers (see the photo on page 92). It feels as though you are walking backwards on the ground, so it is worth trying this on foot first, but ignore strange looks from your friends when you do so!

While you are attaining this position, your horse should not move, so maintain a steady contact on the reins. The rein pressure should increase slightly as you now ask your horse to move with both calves. He should go to move forwards, but do not give the reins yet, maintain the contact. As your horse steps into the reins, he should become aware that you are sitting differently from normal. In this position, with your weight slightly forward, he should feel that the back of your seat is lighter. Keep your knees and thighs close to the saddle to 'close the front door', so that he only has the option to go backwards. With your seat light at the back, you are not in the way of his lumbar muscles working to tuck his haunches under, carrying his body-weight more as he steps backwards. As he takes his first step back, immediately soften the contact slightly to reward him. This has the effect of allowing him to balance through his neck. He should stay softly in your reins, so do not completely drop the contact. Keep your position for three or four steps backward. (Some horses find this exercise 'intellectually' difficult at first. With such horses, one or two steps backward may suffice initially.) Then sit up straight on your seat bones, bring your legs forward again into their normal position and halt. Reward your horse with a gentle pat or your voice, then walk forward again in a straight line.

Rein-back Exercises

Halt square within the parallel poles, making sure that you are equidistant from them when you start. Ask for three or four steps of rein-back, halt and then walk on again. The poles should assist you in walking off straight again after your second halt. Repeat the exercise in both directions to keep your training evenly balanced. Once you can do this exercise from walk to halt, approach the poles in a collected trot. Prepare your horse with half-halts to keep his weight back on his hocks as he halts. The halt should feel that it has energy, or impulsion. Sit very still to keep your horse in a good halt. As you position your legs behind the girth, be careful to give a light aid. As your horse has more energy, he should be more sensitive to your leg aid and react to you changing your seat to its slightly forward position. Again, be ready to soften the contact as soon as you feel him move backwards.

A much more advanced exercise is to ride directly from canter to halt, rein-back, and then go directly into canter again without the second halt, propelling your horse forward. This exercise will be counter-productive unless horse and rider can perform a correct balanced transition from canter to halt. Rein-back to canter is a much easier exercise, which many horses enjoy, and in which the engaging effect of rein-back sets the horse up to make a good transition into canter.

A seesaw exercise is useful for making your and your horse's lumbar muscles more supple. Ride into halt from a collected walk or trot. Ask for four steps of rein-back. Without halting, walk forward again four steps, then go back again, and then halt to finish the seesaw neatly. Think of it as a double-rein back. Next, proceed in trot and you should have lovely elevated, springy steps!

Part III

Remedial Training

Trailer Training

Training horses to load happily is best tackled when the horse is young and impressionable but many older horses have missed out on this and find travelling traumatic.

A good loader is a must for any kind of competition, even local riding club events. However, if you do not plan on competing with your horse, he will probably need to travel at some point in his life, whether going to new and exciting hacking destinations; on holiday; to the vet for x-rays or treatment; to a new yard (barn); or to a new owner. Easy, stress-free loading and travelling will make your life together much safer and happier, so it is worth investing the time in training your horse to load and travel confidently.

If you treat loading as an enjoyable game for your horse, you should have many pleasant years ahead when you can load up and go wherever you like with him. Be aware that older horses might have had bad experiences in the past, so it may take you a little longer to train them. In addition, you will have to match the character of the horse with a suitable trainer: a sensitive horse requires soft, gentle persuasion, whereas a hooligan needs a more dominant approach! Bear in mind that even a strong-minded horse should never be beaten into submission. This causes tension and, if you get a short-term result, in the long run it will be disastrous and you could end up getting hurt. Calm, firm handling is the best approach, particularly when you are on the ground. It is essential to develop a hierarchy between you and your horse, with you as the boss. This is achieved by winning your horse's respect – not by dominating or undermining him.

Preparation

You do not need access to a trailer, lorry or van in the beginning. All you need to do is place two poles parallel to each other 2 m (6½ ft) apart in your schooling arena. Begin by leading your horse with either a stout rope or a lunge line, which offers you a bit more leeway if you encounter any leaping around! Lead your horse around the arena at the end of your usual training session, then between the poles at a steady walk. Stop in between the poles, then walk on again. Practise this a few times during your first session and draw the lesson to a close. Repeat this for the next three or four sessions.

WALKING OVER PLASTIC

Insert a sheet of plastic, which has the advantage of being portable and weather resistant, in between the poles, making sure that you secure both sides of the plastic under the poles. Lead your horse calmly across the plastic. Look forward and expect your horse to follow you. You will reassure your horse by remaining calm and confident and thus encourage him to walk on and follow your positive lead. If he hesitates and pulls back, halt with him, keeping a quiet steady contact on the lead rope. If you pull him, he will pull back and become either anxious or cross, depending on his mentality. Be really determined in your attitude, without getting angry: a healthy positivism is essential in overcoming training problems. When your horse relaxes, soften your body language and walk on again with him. After he responds and follows you again, speak calmly and nicely to him, and pat or rub him so that he knows you are on his side. If he is good, be nice; if he misunderstands, be clear and determined! Be aware that horses are attuned to the smallest shifts in our body language – so if your body language is fearful or defensive, it is a counter-productive giveaway of your feelings. Stand tall, with your chest lifted and shoulders relaxed, rather than crouching in a timid fashion, which sends alarm signals to your horse that there is something to worry about.

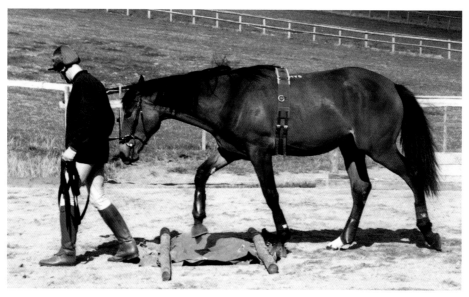

A young horse learning to walk confidently over plastic. Trust between owner and horse needs to be established from the very beginning of the horse's training.

Continue walking over the plastic at the end of your next few training sessions until your horse copes happily with walking over something strange. He should follow you calmly, without you needing to take a firm contact on the lead rope. If your horse feels you grab him, he will probably pull back. A short, quick tug on the rope usually works well to remind him that you are in charge if he decides to test you. Always keep a relaxed, kind contact on the end of the rope, a contact which is just strong enough to ensure that he cannot pull the rope out of your hand.

Progressing to Ramps

The next stage would be to lead him over a sheet of marine plywood, similar to that used for flooring in trailers. Poles either side of the plywod will act as barriers, and two parallel poles in front of the plywood as an 'entrance' will help to guide him over it in a straight line. Practise halting on it, and then walking off it again.

Next, progress to either a lorry (van) or a trailer, remembering that it is best if your horse will load on to both. Make sure that you park your lorry (van) or trailer in a safe, enclosed place. Initially, it helps to park near a fence to discourage horses that step off the side of the ramp, and to bear in mind that a low ramp is less frightening for the first few tries. If you have a trailer, open the front ramp (if it has one) to make it look more inviting and less claustrophobic. Ensure that the chest bar is up and properly secured, so that you do not get dragged out of the other end. If you have a centre partition, release the back of it, push it to one side and check that it is secure and will not accidentally move. If you are at all concerned about your horse, take the partition out. Have a haynet hanging in the front as a tempter, but avoid using food to get your horse into the trailer. Food works for a few times, but you will then find that instead of expecting a reward when he is in, your horse will demand it before he steps on to the ramp. Ponies are particularly good at developing giraffe-like necks, which allow them to reach a bribe while keeping all four feet planted firmly on the ground!

Approach the ramp in the same way you tackled the plastic. Your assistant, if you have one, should stand to one side of the trailer near the ramp. Walk calmly and determinedly up the ramp, expecting your horse to follow you. He should trust you by now and march smartly up beside you. If this works, stand with him holding the rope in a relaxed manner.

If your horse stops to look, or puts his feet on the ramp and will not go any further, keep looking ahead and stop with him, maintaining a steady contact on the rope. If you have a bossy horse, carry a schooling whip, rather than have someone behind him with a big stick, because this generally causes more problems. If you will be travelling primarily on your own, you need to practise loading on your own but, in the early stages, it helps to have a calm, confident assistant to open and close the ramps for you and to be on hand for moral support and to help you catch him should he break free.

If your horse refuses to budge, a sharp tap on his hindquarters should encourage him to walk on. As soon as he walks forward one step, relax the rope. If you pull on the rope he will pull back. Your horse should then work out that it is nicer to go forward than backwards. Praise him when he is good and, again, stand firm if he rebels. Patience is imperative, so allow plenty of time to deal with a hesitant or pushy horse.

If your horse gets a bit clever and leaps away, dragging you with him, be forearmed by leading him with a lunge rein, which gives you much more leeway. Do not let go; instead, use short, sharp tugs to regain his attention. Once he stands calmly, repeat the loading procedure again.

When he is standing still inside the trailer your assistant should quietly secure the centre partition and tail rail. If you are on your own, make sure your horse will stand quietly tied up on his own before you move around to the back of the trailer to close and secure the ramp. Talk to him as you do this so he does not think you have disappeared. The ramp must not be slammed up suddenly, or your horse may be scared. If he is still calm, the ramp should be gently closed and secured. Reassure him, and give him a few minutes to get used to being inside the trailer. Ask your assistant to quietly open the front ramp, and release the chest bar, securing the partition to give a wider exit if possible. If you are on your own, he will have to stand quietly on his own while you do this yourself. Untie your horse and lead him out, giving him plenty of time to look at where he is putting his feet. Making sure your assistant is out of the way, quietly lead your horse out down the front ramp of the trailer. Take things slowly. You do not want him to rush out and barge past you. Once unloaded reward your horse for his excellent behaviour. Praise him and offer him his favourite food or titbits so that he thinks he has just had a wonderful experience. Repeat this procedure two or three times a week until he will happily stand inside on his own with both ramps secured.

When your horse loads and unloads happily, go for a short drive taking your assistant with you. When you arrive back home, unload in the same calm and positive fashion. Be relaxed and try to enjoy the whole process and make a fuss of him with his favourite food and treats when he gets back. This approach will keep you both calm when you go to shows, competitions, the vet or even on holiday together.

Ultimately, travelling should be stress free for both you and your horse, which means that you will arrive at your destination ready for anything!

Working with the Older Horse

It is important to assess each individual case carefully when working with older horses. An older horse is stiffer and less agile than a young horse and requires careful warming up before exercise and can quickly lose his confidence if the surface he is working on is poor and he is unsure of where he is putting his feet. Knowing and understanding your older horse is the best guide to his work. They all appreciate a quiet hack (although some older horses think otherwise and prefer to gallop) and those who spook for fun will always have a tendency to do so, to show off and enjoy the moment!

Lungeing

When lungeing the older horse, keep the circle you are working on fairly big and walk around on a small circle yourself to keep a close contact with him. Remember that he will not be able to perform circles that are too small for him and if asked to do so will worry and become unbalanced. Spend a fair amount of time in walk, making transitions between walk and halt until your older horse is supple enough to trot. Canter work on the lunge must be used with care. Only if you have an experienced and well-balanced 'oldie' should you do any canter work at all.

Lungeing over poles for short spells should help him to maintain some elasticity in his joints. It is the same with us – unless we use our bodies, they become more and more stiff and restricted, so it is important to keep your older horse active and alert. Good exercise will be beneficial to his mental wellbeing as well as his physical state. Some horses will always be more willing to work than others, simply due to differences in their character and disposition. It all boils down to knowing your horse and what he needs for a healthy and happy life.

Dealing with 'Former Careers'

Thoroughbreds who have raced in their younger days will quite often still be acting as though they are 'ready for the off' at thirty – exactly as they were at three. Ex-hurdlers will try to keep hurdling and sometimes they will not understand that they do not have to launch into orbit three strides out over a 10 cm (4 in) pole on the ground. If you are retraining a racehorse, it is much fairer to do it when your horse is young enough to adapt. Once horses are over fifteen, compromises have to be made in their training as they are sometimes too set in their ways, especially if they have spent all their life being ridden one way and you come along and expect something entirely different. For example, hurdlers are often encouraged to take off as soon as they are close enough to clear the hurdle – which might be 3.5 m (11½ ft) or more away. Trying to retrain them to collect and come in closer can be just too mind-blowing for them.

Older dressage horses will still enjoy performing their 'party pieces' whatever age they are. They might not be able to do as well as they did in their younger days, but if you make allowances for that, they will be happy horses and should always believe that they are still the best at what they do.

Pole Work

Pole work is excellent for older horses if they have become accustomed to it throughout their lives. If they have not, it is worth trying to walk over a single pole to see how your horse copes. He might appreciate a bit of variety, but if he really becomes confused or is too stiff to cope, then it is best left alone.

Be vigilant about any mental or physical problems and aware of how your older horse is going. If you have had him for many years, you should have developed a strong enough partnership to understand when he has had enough of a particular exercise or if he is not in the mood and cheating like mad! Warm your older horse up in walk until you see or feel him relax. With ridden work, some lateral movements in walk should help him to loosen up. Half-halts and transitions between walk and halt will make him more alert. Always begin with large circles and easy turns to get his confidence. If he is too stiff at first to go over poles, ride patterns in between them. Set the poles out in parallel pairs around the school. You can make transitions between the poles, circle around them and generally use them as a focal point to help accuracy. Just because your horse is older does not mean that you can drift aimlessly around the arena. Your horse will appreciate positive, clear instructions from you. Always begin with good stretching. An older horse will not be able to come out of his stable and stretch down to the floor. He might give you a halfway stretch, which is fine. As he becomes freer through his work he should be able to stretch down further. Use the stretching at frequent intervals, particularly toward the end of your training session to test if your work has been correct. This is important for all horses of any age.

When riding an older horse, remember to come off his back now and again into a forward seat, taking your weight on the stirrups rather than just sitting on him. This will help his muscles ease and prevent stiffness.

It is important to be able to take your weight off your horse's back to ease his muscles.

Collection

The older horse also needs to be able work in a degree of collection, i.e. taking his weight on his hocks and lightening his forehand. This helps his entire body to become stronger by working him in balance. He needs to preserve his self-carriage to alleviate leg problems. If older horses work continually on their forehands, they can easily develop front leg injuries and wear and tear of the bones and joints. If you can train your older horse to work correctly with his weight balanced between his hindquarters and his forehand, like a pair of scales with you as the balancing pole in the middle, you will help to preserve his physical state, and may even improve it.

Bucking and Rearing

While Pony Clubbers might think that bucking and rearing are great fun, adult riders tend to take a different view!

Many horses buck when they feel good and the conditions are right: they are fit, keen to go and the ground is soft and the air is cool. What better way to express your happiness than by packing a few bucks as you move into the first canter out hacking, or when you have just popped a log and are tremendously pleased with yourself? Sometimes, if a horse does not have enough turnout, of if he is schooled into the ground, he might buck when out hacking simply because he is thrilled to be doing something different in the open air. While it is almost impossible to stop the occasional 'wahoo' buck, other causes of bucking can be dealt with. Similarly, it is nearly impossible to cure a hardened rearer but, if the problem is caught in time – when the horse is at a trainable and malleable age – it can be reduced or eliminated.

Possible Causes

With both problems it is always best to check for pain: have your vet check your horse's teeth, back and general development and a qualified saddler check your horse's saddle. Think about the bit you use and how you use it – many riders move on to stronger bits if their horses get a bit fresh, rather than working on their riding skills or reviewing stable management. It is worth investigating factors like your horse's diet and turnout; if he is not happy in his daily routine he will never be a responsive ride, and if he is giddy through being over-fed, you are both an accident waiting to happen. Try to take a holistic look at these problems rather than just dealing with the possible result, i.e. bucking and rearing.

Having eliminated all of the possible pain problems and stable management issues, horses that have developed serious rearing or bucking problems need to be taken back to basics and patiently worked through their problems. You have to decide at the outset whether your horse acts in this way out of malice or out of frustration. A horse with a tendency to rear can have over-developed under-neck muscles, which he uses to lift his head really high and then stand up. The horse who bucks is good at getting his head low and pulling down onto his forehand in order to get his back end off the floor. Again, provided there is no physical reason for this behaviour, and it does not stem from ill-fitting tack or bad riding, there are ways in which poles can help to solve these problems.

Problem Management

It is best to keep your problem horse at home. While there are many training facilities available, sending your horse away is never the final solution because ultimately the two of you need to work in partnership. Yes, someone else might be able to retrain your horse and stop him from bucking or rearing, but if you have not changed your approach to your horse – and probably your riding and handling skills – the original problems will resurface within a few weeks and you will then be back at the beginning, a frustrated (and poorer) owner of an equally unhappy horse. If you are locked in a battle with your horse it is important to recognize that you both need to change in order to move your relationship forward.

If your horse's behaviour is malicious, be sure that you have the expertise to deal with him and to stick with his training through some potentially very difficult (and possibly scary) times. If you have any doubts about your abilities, be sensible and ask for help from a professional trainer who you trust and who will help you. If your horse is frustrated and confused, the root of the problem might be that you misunderstand each other, which generally happens when a rider inadvertently gives a horse the wrong signals. Again, if you are nervous around, or afraid of, your horse, he will feel insecure, which will result in threatening behaviour if he is the type to take advantage with his strength. The bold, intelligent horses who are a pleasure at eight can be absolute monsters when they are three, four and five! My own horse was called Damien as a foal because he was a little devil, but has matured into a (reasonably) sensible ten-year-old.

Retraining

If you feel confident to retrain your horse, begin with the basics.

RE-ESTABLISHING A RELATIONSHIP
For your own safety, always work a problem horse from the ground, either in hand or on the lunge. Wear gloves and a hard hat and, if it makes you

feel more confident, a body protector. Continue your training in the yard by making sure that you handle your horse in a **calm, confident and controlled** way at all times. You must be the boss, so think, act and ultimately believe it. It is counter-productive to rush to the yard straight from work anxious about the little time you have; if you are anxious, your horse will sense your unease and take every opportunity to act up, preying on your frustrations and pushing you to the limit. Even if your time is limited, you have to pretend to your horse that you have all the time in the world but do not tackle new problems unless you do have the time, because these situations always take a lot longer to resolve than you think they will. Build up trust in the stable, too. Your horse must earn rewards, not have them doled out on demand. If you are too free with treats, your horse will get pushy and arrogant and bully you for titbits. Use treats to reward good behaviour, like standing still to be groomed and tacked up.

Try not to let your horse use you as a rubbing post. A lot of people take this as a sign of affection, but horses are not cats! Rubbing against you can turn into pushing you about if you have a bossy horse. It is a lot easier and safer to handle and tack up a horse who stands respectfully for you. I know of one rider who had three broken toes, a wrecked Achilles tendon, a cracked rib and numerous visits to an osteopath over a six-month period because of her bargy youngster. Needless to say, this should not have happened in the first place!

LUNGEING

Once your relationship is re-established, begin lungeing as described on pages 27–34. The chambon is the best aid to use because it is not restrictive once the horse lowers his neck and stretches. All horses need to relax through their backs first before proceeding further.

When you have established the basics, set three or four poles in a fan shape. Lunge your horse over these in walk. Keep to the inner side of the poles for walk as they are closer together towards the inside edge of the fan (about 0.8 m or 2½ ft apart). Once your horse is keeping a good rhythm and bend as he works over the fan of poles, progress to trot, always working him on both reins. Use the chambon for a good few weeks in these sessions with both rearers and buckers. Use a roller (surcingle) as opposed to a saddle for the lunge work to eliminate any risk of tension in your horse's back. This is also handy if your horse decides to try the ultimate refusal and roll; if he rolls in his saddle and breaks the tree the replacement cost could be horren- dous – never mind the wear and tear on your vocal cords as you shout at

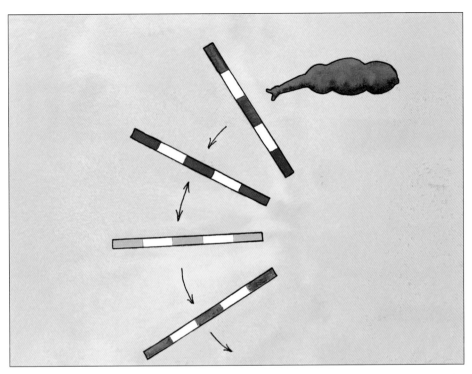

Poles set out in a fan. The distance between the middle of each pole should be approximately 1.3 m (4 ft).

him. A roller also lets you watch his back muscles working. They should visibly contract and expand like big elastic bands once your horse is going correctly and this will be accentuated when he is working over the poles. By setting the poles as a fan, your horse will be encouraged to work in a bend to the inside of the lunge circle. This will help him rediscover softness, which is harder to re-establish with straight-line pole work, and discourage him from setting his neck either too high (rearing) or too low (bucking). Once your horse is relaxed and bending correctly he should forget about misbehaving.

A rearer is best worked in a chambon which will discourage him from lifting his head too high in the first place, and encourage him to stretch down and relax through his back. If you use side reins, elasticized side reins will help him to stay calm and not feel claustrophobic with a contact. Begin with just the outside one attached until you are sure he will accept the contact happily. Do not have them so long that your horse could find a way to lift his head really high, because there is the danger of him going up and over backwards. Conversely, if the side reins are too short, your horse will tense up all over again and panic, taking you both back to square one. If this happens, you must start all over again, which could take months.

A bucker will probably be happier in side reins than a rearer. Try to avoid reins with soft elastic inserts, as a bucker will probably pull at them. Once he works out that he can pull against the reins and they will yield to him, he may well do the same with you on top, pulling your arms forward and resuming bucking because he can pull his head down. Plain leather or webbing reins are best as they limit what a horse can do to avoid softening his back and taking weight behind.

Continue working on curved lines with the poles in both cases. If the circle becomes smaller as a horse becomes more flexible, you may need to shorten the inside side rein a little to maintain a correct bend from the head to the tail. Once the pole work is good on curves, then try a series of parallel trotting poles, working up to six or eight. This will help your horse to develop the correct top line muscles and make it difficult for him to rear, as the incorrect muscles will now be weaker and your horse happier to work correctly. A horse prone to bucking needs to relax and be freer through his back muscles. He often has strong muscles in his quarters and back, but tension causes him to buck rather than work through his back. It can take from six to nine months to get to this stage with some horses – unfortunately, it takes as long as it takes and there are no shortcuts.

Back in the Saddle

Once your horse performs well on the lunge, you must determine whether it is now safe for you to ride. Assess this from the horse's general demeanour and his confidence in his work, and in you. If he is now calm, confident and happy in his work with you, then repeat the whole training process from the saddle. Introduce the saddle on the lunge at some point, so that it is not a big shock to your horse when you get on. You are really breaking-in your horse all over again, to fill in any earlier gaps in his training and your handling. This is essential for your own safety and your future relationship with your horse.

Rushing

Rushing can put both horse and rider in a dangerous situation. It is both uncomfortable for the horse and damaging to his muscles if he is allowed to work like this over a long period of time. Rushing around out of control destroys the rider's confidence in the horse, and may well destroy their relationship altogether. Horses that tend to rush can panic when faced with a sequence of poles or jumps, so the best way to tackle this problem is on a circle. Set the poles out in a star shape. Keep the star big, so that you do not turn the horse on a tight circle, as this may well wind him up.

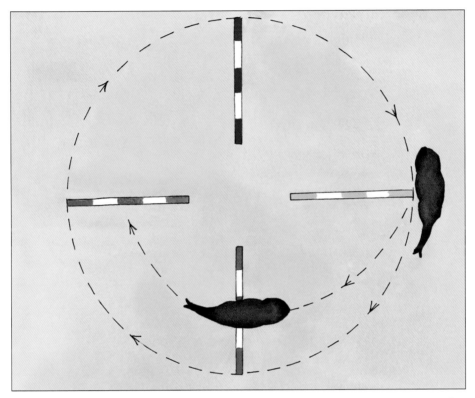

Poles in a large star shape. Begin by riding around the outside on a large circle, then spiral in, riding over each one in turn.

Re-establishing an Outline and Control

Walk a big circle around the outside of the poles to establish a bend through the horse's body. Keep him listening to your inside leg near the girth, so that he steps into your outside rein. Control his haunches with your outside leg behind the girth. Try not to pull at him if he goes too fast, but to keep a steady, firm outside rein. Keep your inside elbow flexible so that you can keep some elasticity in the contact to prevent the horse throwing himself against the reins with his head up and his back hollow. Keeping a feel on the inside rein like this helps to calm the horse, and makes him think about your rein aid, rather than panicking about it. Your outside hand must stay still, and on no account seesaw on the bit. This causes a sore mouth and a horse with a tense jaw, who runs away as soon as he feels any pressure on his mouth. The horse needs to relax the muscles under his neck, which become tense if he is trying to avoid working in an outline. This is a sign of a tense, tight back, and a reluctance to work in a more relaxed, rounder outline with a swinging back. Some horses only have to see a pole or jump to cause them to rush. By introducing poles into the schooling as a controlling exercise as opposed to jumping them at speed, the horse changes his attitude to poles, and does not charge at them any more. Ride in a very matter-of-fact way, and try not to react yourself when approaching a pole on the ground. Keep breathing normally, and keep your seat muscles relaxed. Keep a steady leg contact to keep the horse straight and a calm, steady contact on the reins. You should be able to move your fingers if you want to, to keep them relaxed but avoid fiddling around with the contact, otherwise the horse will tense his mouth.

A horse that rushes away from the rider works with a hollow back and raised neck. This results in the underneath muscles of the neck becoming over-developed, making it easier to pull against the rider's hands.

HALF-HALTS
As you get parallel to each pole with your shoulders, half-halt. Repeat this several times until you feel the horse start to relax and become rounder through his back. This may take up to twenty minutes if the horse is very stressed. If this is as far as you get on the first few training sessions, that is

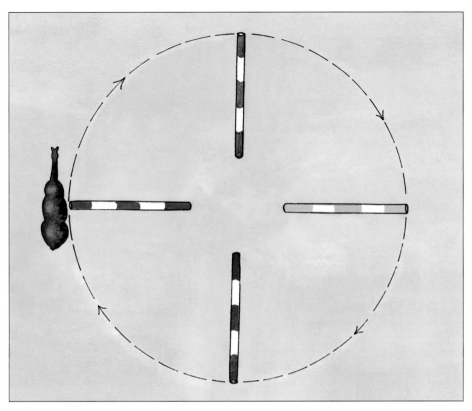

Half-halting when you are parallel to the end of each pole.

fine because relaxation is the most important thing to establish. The horse
must understand that you can stop him with your whole body and not the
reins alone.

Once your horse is accepting the half-halts, alternate between riding in
walk around one pole, then over the next. This keeps variety in the exercise
and the horse is less likely to switch off and run away. Keep the sessions
calm and not too long. You have to establish the half-halts and the small
circles, but feel when the horse is a bit tired and do not wear him out,
otherwise tension creeps back in again. Remember to work equally on both
reins.

Again, stay calm, and make sure that you avoid tensing up. You need to
be firm in your position, keeping yourself solid and secure, but without
being tense and hanging on to the reins. The aim is to be able to soften the
rein contact without the horse running away again. Continue trying to
soften the tone of your arm muscles, so that you can lighten the contact
without dropping it altogether. Repeat the half-halts as frequently as you
need to, to keep the horse listening to you.

This mare has learnt over several months to relax the underneath of her neck by correct riding in a snaffle bit. The next stage is to build up the crest muscles more to even out the neck muscle development.

INTRODUCING LATERAL STEPS ON A CIRCLE

Try keeping a slight leg-yield feeling of stepping sideways around the circumference of the circle from one pole to the next. As you pass the end of a pole, turn your upper body and the horse's forehand in the direction of the centre of the circle, keeping his body on an angle of thirty degrees to the circumference of the circle. Support him with your outside rein and keep your inside rein soft. Keep your weight on your inside seat bone. Ask him to step sideways with your inside leg near the girth, and your outside leg back to prevent his quarters swinging out too much. He will take sideways steps with his legs crossing, as in a leg-yield (see page 165) with his tail towards the outside of the circle, travelling in a sideways direction towards the outside end of the next pole. Lateral steps on a circle help to discourage the horse from rushing away, as he is focused towards the inside of the circle.

Avoid drifting in towards the middle of the star. Straighten up and ride the next segment with no lateral steps. Alternate the segments between each pole as you ride around the large circle. Intersperse this with small circles around the poles to keep the horse really listening to *you*. Maintain a steady walk throughout.

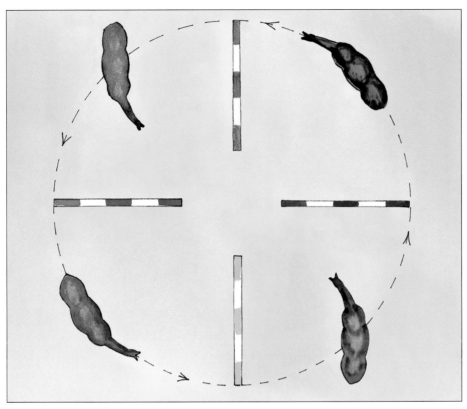

Alternate the segments between each pole as you ride around the large circle. Ride one segment with lateral steps, and the next segment straight.

INTRODUCING TROT AND CANTER

Once you have got to this stage, introduce a steady rising trot. Resume the big circle as in the beginning and half-halt at the end of each pole again. Then go around alternate poles, bypassing the other two, but half-halting as you do so. If this is successful on both reins, have a rest in walk. Then ride rising trot over the alternate poles, and sit for the two small circles. This will help you both develop better balance and control whether rising or sitting. Frequent relaxation on a long rein is advisable to give you both a mental break as quite a lot of concentration is needed to keep calm.

The next stage is to walk in an even rhythm over the four poles. Then do the same in trot altering the distance between the poles to 1.3 m (4 ft). Avoid canter work until the trot work is calm and relaxed. Usually, if you prepare the horse well at walk and trot, the canter is usually no longer a problem, as you have already corrected the outline, your aids, and the relaxation of you both.

Then place random, individual poles around the school and ride over them in walk and trot as though they were invisible. If your horse does not feel you tense up at all, he will remain calm and steady. Introduce canter when you have really established a controlled, calm attitude in walk and trot.

Advanced In-hand Work

This is best done after lungeing your horse first to relax him and warm up his muscles. It is helpful to do a little in-hand work before mounting up, and it can help to engage the hocks and lift the horse's back.

You need to work the horse from the bridle, i.e. in some circumstances having a lunge line attached to the bit, or working with your normal reins. Long reins are a good idea if you are proficient at using them without tripping yourself up; remember to take your spurs off first! In-hand work is like riding the horse from the ground. The added advantage is that you can see how the horse is using himself, and it helps you to develop a good rapport between you.

Transitions

Begin by walking around the whole arena on the left side of your horse with your hands holding the bridle reins as though you were riding. The outside rein needs to be across his neck by his withers, held in your right hand, and the left rein in your left hand. Walk by the horse's shoulder, with a long schooling whip in your right hand as well, so that you can tap him on his inside hind leg to activate it if you need to. Walk and halt transitions are best to start with. Stand up straight, as though you were riding him and use your reins exactly as you would when sitting in the saddle; keep his head at arm's length to keep him away from you and maintain his straightness with your outside rein.

Leading the horse with the left arm outstretched and holding the outside rein and whip with the right hand.

Walk alongside him with your body towards him so that you can watch what he is doing. He should respond to your voice command to 'walk-on' and to stop also. The aids are a combination of body, rein, whip and voice. Make sure you are consistent with your voice aid, so decide beforehand which words you are going to use and stick to them. Where applicable, use the same words as when lungeing. Your horse will quickly learn word association. He should walk-on voluntarily from your voice. If he does not, give him a quick tap with the whip. Soften the reins when he responds. If he does not want to stop with you, use your outside rein more firmly, and block him by standing firmly on the ground, as though rooted to the spot. If you just use the rein alone, you may well be towed along! Apply the same correct 'half-halt' posture as when mounted, to maintain your stance on the ground.

Standing Square

For this exercise, place two or three poles end to end on the inside of the track on the long side of the school. Leave enough room for the horse to walk down between the fence and the poles. You need to stay on the other side of the poles away from the horse.

Use the lunge line and have side reins on your horse to maintain his outline. They should not be too short which will cause tension in his neck, or too long, which will defeat the object of having them at all! Attach the lunge line to a lunge cavesson over the bridle if your horse is fairly obedient, or if you are new to this.

Carry a long schooling whip. An old lunge whip with the lash chopped off at about six inches is adequate, unless you feel like investing in a driving whip, or piaffe whip. You need a long shaft with a short lash. This allows you to reach the hind legs with the whip while standing out of range of the hooves. If you are working with a friend, they could lead the horse while you work him.

Ask the horse to halt. If he is not standing square, tap the offending leg gently with the end of the whip. You want the horse to pick his foot up and replace it in a better position. Praise him if he does it, repeat the tap if he does not. Try this with each foot in turn, so that he can pick up and replace each one without panicking or kicking out. If he kicks out at you, give him a quick sharp tap on the offending leg. Quietly ask him again more gently. He should have worked out that if he does it gently he is praised, if he kicks, he gets another tap. Treat sensitive horses with patience. They may be frightened of the whip because of some past experience, so tactful handling is called for and careful handling of the whip. Have some sugar lumps, or his favourite treat, in your pocket to reward him when he understands. If he tries to walk off, a firm half-halt on the line will tell him not to. You need the line to jangle the bit or cavesson, so as to make a noise with it rather than to inflict a harsh jab, which would worry him.

Asking the horse to pick up each hind leg in turn.

The result you are looking for is that your horse stands square on all four feet. Having the poles in a line helps to keep him straight, and to deter him from swinging his haunches towards you. He should begin to look rounder just behind the saddle, and his haunches should look a bit more tucked under, especially if you can persuade him to step more under his body with his hind legs in the halt.

Once he understands, lead him away around the school, then repeat the exercise on the other rein. Finish without the side reins, lungeing him in a relaxed trot with a stretch.

Lateral Steps

Set the poles out in a big star shape, with enough room for you to work between and around them. Bring him onto a big circle around the poles. Give yourself enough room so that you do not trip over, so be aware all the time of the location of the poles. Between the first two poles, walk a normal

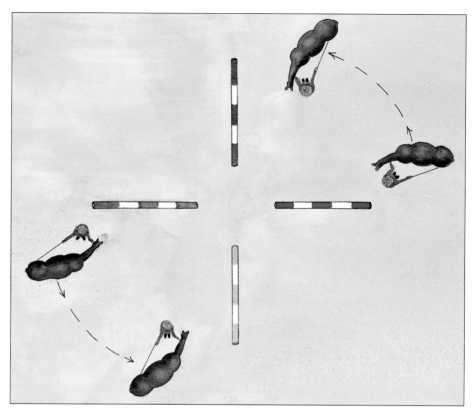

Working the horse in-hand, moving laterally between the poles.

circle line. As you get to the end of the second pole, keep a firmer outside rein, and tap his inside hind leg with the whip if necessary to move his body away from you in a leg-yield. Keep your inside arm outstretched to move him away from you towards the third pole. Then straighten up, and go straight towards the fourth, continuing on your circle. Ask for the lateral steps at the fourth pole. Repeat the exercise on the other rein and finish with a relaxed walk together around the arena.

Balking, Napping and Spookiness

Balking, napping and spookiness can be a problem with some horses. They are usually the clever ones who think and question things. Sometimes horses are genuinely scared by something and the natural response is to jump away and to stare at whatever it is straight on with ears sharply pricked. Even a goat can grow into a dragon in these circumstances! There is usually a reason for this behaviour. The horse may be reacting to a nervous rider; he picks up the fear from the rider, and leaps around when he cannot handle it any longer. This then frightens the rider even more and the horse reacts even more. This is a dangerous situation to be in. If the rider cannot break this catch-22 situation, horse and rider are both heading for trouble, either becoming totally out of control, or, at worst, having an accident.

Alternatively, the horse may be just misunderstanding what he is being asked. Always check first whether there is a physical problem behind the horse's behaviour, e.g. an ill-fitting saddle or a sore mouth, before retraining him. Also be aware of your own reactions when he is misbehaving. You may be winding him up if you are tense or angry. There may also be short-term spookiness or a refusal to co-operate, arising from a new environment or following a period off work after injury. If the cause is none of the above and you still have a problem, he needs to be taught to cope with his anxiety. Whether this occurs while jumping, resulting in him slamming the brakes on and refusing to jump, for various reasons, or refusing to hack out, for example, the training is the same.

Obstacle Courses

Returning to pole work, put poles randomly around the arena. The odd plastic block placed between them to circle around is a good idea. You may also raise the poles off the floor with something safe, such as plastic blocks, or use sturdy cavalletti. The horse needs to take notice of the obstacle course you are setting out. If it is too flimsy, or the objects are too close together, he may throw in the towel and refuse to co-operate, even bulldozing through things!

Set out a simple, clear course. The sheet of plastic that was used for the trailer training will come in handy again at a later stage!

Lunge the horse first, to alleviate stiffness and prepare him mentally. If he will not lunge, some simple in-hand work will be as good.

Then, ride him around the arena as best you can, remaining calm and in control. Aim to get him into a deep round outline using frequent half-halts. If he is still very tense, this may take a while, and trying to hurry it may be counter-productive. Keep a calm, steady contact on the reins to reassure him. Begin by walking around a plastic block or a cone. Repeat this in either direction a few times. Then go off for a bit of trot work to encourage him to go forward. Rising trot will probably be best but when he is relaxed

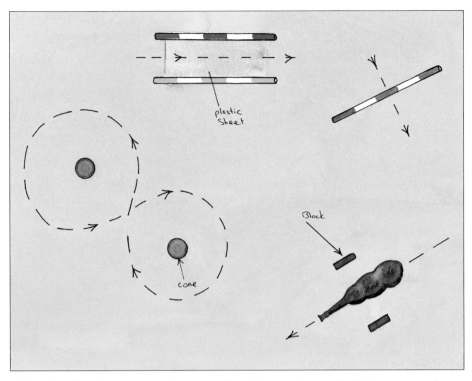

A simple obstacle course to keep your horse's attention and add interest to the training session.

through his back, introduce sitting trot as well as he has to learn to go forward with you sitting in the saddle eventually. If he balks and does not respond well to your leg aid, then repeat the leg aid faster and stronger, followed by a sharp tap with your schooling whip just behind your leg. The whip is to be used as an extra leg, rather than a punishment. When you want the horse to go forward from your leg, make sure that you stay relaxed in your seat muscles, so as not to block the forward movement when it occurs. Also, lighten the contact to almost nothing so that he does not feel restricted in any way. Give him no excuse not to go forward. The idea is to isolate your leg aid so that he takes more notice of it.

Once he listens, praise him, and go to the next obstacle, a pole to walk over for example. Do all the obstacle work in walk first, but progress to trot if it is more helpful for you both. You have to remain flexible in your attitude when dealing with balky, spooky horses, and build up a repertoire of tricks of your own to outwit him! It is a matter of being cleverer than the horse, rather than continually telling him off.

In a future session, with the poles raised off the ground, ride alongside them first. Then go around them in a series of circles. If you raise two parallel poles, to simulate a channel, or tunnel, you can ride between them. Introduce other patterns, such as serpentines or figures of eight. Intersperse each exercise with riding the horse forward. The occasional small jump will help him to pop over calmly. Try just turning in off a trot circle and taking the jump, as though it is no 'big deal'. Return to your school movements in between each obstacle, to keep him interested. He should begin to relax. After a few sessions, there should be a big difference in his attitude. It is all about putting the fun element back into his training, so there is no reason for him to balk.

This rider is maintaining a focused, calm attitude while the horse comes to terms with the 'spooky' pole.

The odd leap due to high spirits is understandable, but anything done with tension or malice needs to be dealt with quickly and calmly, and not be allowed to develop into a bad habit. This can happen with young horses, so just remain calm, secure in your attitude and opposition, and they should settle fairly easily. With older horses who are more set in their ways it is a tougher job to undertake, so only tackle the problem if you are sure you can do it, otherwise it is best to get some professional help from someone who will teach you how to cope with your horse. Sending him away for training is only of benefit if you go too. Unless you learn how to do it yourself, the old problems return once the horse is back home.

Simple obstacle work can restore your own confidence as it gives you something else to concentrate on, apart from worrying about your horse.

Progress is usually quick, and you will both develop a calmer, more controlled attitude to strange situations. If your horse is balky when out hacking, return to the schoolwork. Once you have him listening again over a period if time, anything from a couple of weeks to a couple of months, them quietly return to going out. Always begin in walk again, so that he does not get wound up by going too fast too soon. Hacking should be relaxation, not bombing madly around the countryside! Go out with someone you trust who has a calm, reliable horse. Do not risk undoing all your good work in an instant otherwise you will have to start all over again!

Crookedness: Fault Correction

Crookedness applies to riding on circles as well as straight lines, and applies as much to the rider as it does to the horse! Working on straightness is covered on pages 58–61. This section tackles fault correction.

A horse can be crooked laterally, i.e. one who has difficulty following the tracks of his front feet with his hind feet when travelling on straight lines or circles. The result is an inability to perform any movement correctly as he has no co-ordination between his front and back ends. He often characteristically twists his head and neck to compensate and ends up like a corkscrew. A crooked horse then affects his rider. Unless a rider is aware of their position and is very good at maintaining an upright, straight posture, they are, in turn, affected by the horse, and will be made to sit to one side where it is most comfortable for the crooked horse, resulting in a crooked saddle and back problems for both horse and rider.

Conversely, a crooked rider who is very stuck in their ways and collapsed down one side of their body can make the horse lop-sided. It is like carrying a heavy shopping bag on the same arm all the time: you quickly become stiff on one side and collapsed on the other. Problems of crookedness can be compounded if both horse and rider are naturally crooked in the same direction.

Correct Contact

Horses can be crooked in a different way, i.e. longitudinally unbalanced. Keeping a horse straight depends on the ability of the rider to maintain the correct contact for the horse's standard of training. This correct contact is important, but it is hard for even a skilful rider to keep an even contact on a seriously crooked horse.

The feeling of contact is determined by the stage of the horse's education and his ability to work through his back and hindquarters. A horse working incorrectly will be on his forehand and consequently leans on the rider's hands. Many horses are quite content to be 'held up' by the rider but a rider with an insecure seat will probably be pulled forward out of balance as a result. To correct this heavy feeling, use half-halts to ask the horse to take his weight on his hind legs to adjust his balance so that he does not need to lean on the reins. You will feel a softening of the reins as your horse arches his neck in front of you and his back lifts up underneath you. At precisely this moment you must soften your whole body (just the tone changes, not the posture) and allow your horse to remain quietly on the bit. Sit passively, without collapsing, and let him enjoy what he is doing. This pleasant sensation is his reward.

If your horse is heavy on the reins, increase your seat and leg aids to match. If he lightens the feeling on the reins correctly, then soften your aids. However, if he has loosened the reins by tucking in his chin and evading the contact, take up the slack and keep your legs on to take him forwards to the bridle. Ensure that the horse does not get into the habit of going overbent and behind the bit. Within a few steps he should soften his jaw, allowing you to soften the reins again. A light contact must come from your horse softening himself to you, not by him demanding that you give him the reins whenever he feels like it. The more balanced your horse, the lighter your reins become, reaching the point where you can yield the reins completely and your horse will stay in balance without relying on them at all.

Exercises to Help Maintain the Correct Contact and Straightness

Keep this balanced feeling over a line of poles spaced at trot-distance apart (approximately 1.3 m or 4 ft); you should now find it a lot easier to remain straight both longitudinally and laterally.

Next, try riding a circle around an object like a plastic cone, using the cone as a focal point. Your horse should turn in balance with you. Make sure you do not use too much inside rein at this point and spoil the even contact. The horse should soften into your inside rein if he is stepping correctly into your outside rein. To allow the horse to bend, the outside rein has to give sufficiently to allow the outside of the horse to stretch through the turn. The contact on both reins should feel fairly even. If you can feel this, he is now straight. To finish, lengthen your reins to allow him to stretch down into a longer rein so he ends up relaxed and with a swinging back. Doing this exercise on both reins is necessary to compare the difference (if any) between both sides of the horse. If the horse disappears altogether from your inside rein contact, this may indicate that he is yielding *too easily* in this direction, i.e. he is still concave on this side and convex on the other side.

As a test of your straightness, ride between two parallel poles and halt. If you can halt square from walk, trot and canter, you have a straight horse! This takes a bit of practice, but is necessary in the dressage arena, because all tests require you to ride straight down the centre line and halt square, so you must get this right. Place the poles on the centre line to check that you can ride a straight centre line. Then place them across the centre, as the middle of a figure of eight.

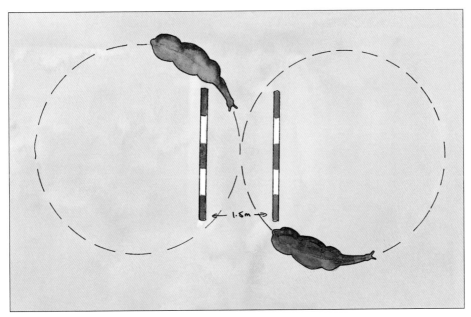

Figure of eight with the poles 1.5 m (5 ft) apart. Make sure you are sitting straight as you ride between them.

Think of the figure of eight as two 20 m circles joined up at the centre point of the school. Between the two poles you should have three or four strides of walk. If you are riding through them in trot, you need to trot before the poles and continue after them for a stride or two to give yourself time to prepare for the transitions on a straight line. When riding this in canter, make sure that you make a good transition down to either trot or walk to change the canter lead. You could pass through the poles in canter without changing direction a couple of times to check your own position in the saddle before making a change of rein.

Riding between the poles to check straightness.

Crookedness often reflects differential degrees of suppleness and stiffness in the muscles and associated tissues on either side of the horse. It can take some time and a good deal of work to make a horse truly symmetrical.

Part IV

Jumping Schooling

The Jumping Seat

The jumping, or light, seat enables you to remain in balance with your horse when jumping obstacles and travelling at speed. It also gives you extra security in the saddle in case anything untoward should happen. This will be explained below.

If your horse jumps over poles or other obstacles with a tight, hollow back, he could pull muscles in his neck or back, so it is important to be aware of the outline and the suppleness of his back at all times. By riding in a correct jumping seat, you will help him to achieve this.

The Balanced Forward Seat

It is advisable to shorten your stirrups three or four holes when jumping, to allow your thighs to lie snugly against the saddle, with your knees supported by the knee roll of the jumping saddle. You have an extremely efficient security system with your thighs in front of your upper body, especially when your weight is on the balls of your feet with a deeply flexed heel. It is important to develop the ability to keep your weight down through the whole leg so you do not lose a stirrup by inadvertently raising your knee or heel. Your lower leg should remain underneath you at all times. This lower leg position is crucial to staying in balance with your horse.

When approaching an obstacle, your backside should be in contact with the saddle. With your upper body upright or very slightly in front of the vertical, sit upright on your seat bones in the same way as you do in the dressage seat.

Practise this forward seat over poles to start with, from a balanced canter. Make sure you can stay in balance without

The jumping seat enables the rider to feel balanced and in control without hindering the horse or using the reins for support.

relying on the reins, or leaning on the horse's neck for support. Once you are happy with this, proceed to single poles raised on blocks. Build up to a sequence of two or three small jumps in a grid, set at about 6.5 m (21 ft) apart for one non-jumping stride between each.

CONTROL

You should be able to use the small of your back to control your horse in conjunction with both your reins and, conversely, to swing with his movement with a supple waist so you do not hinder your horse's canter stride. Sit up tall in the saddle – think of stretching and firming your abdominal muscles to support your lower back. To balance your horse you must first perfect half-halts in the jumping seat. By bracing the small of your back and closing your knees on to the saddle, you become immovable from waist to knees. By thinking of closing your knees together, the lower part of your thigh and the upper part of your calf should be brought more securely on to your horse's sides, giving you a solid lower body position without increasing the weight on your backside. This posture is very useful not just in the context of jumping, but also when controlling keen horses in the open. The reason why so many riders are unable to control their horses in the faster gaits is that they do not ride like this. It is not necessary to dig your backside into the saddle or to lean backwards against the reins. Both of these reactions will make your horse hollow his back, hindering his bascule.

The outside rein may also be required in the half-halt to check your horse's forward motion briefly. The half-halt should last only as long as it takes to make one stride and then be softened. If the half-halt lasts for longer than this you run the risk of your horse leaning on your contact. You want your horse to take his weight on his hocks and lower his croup, resulting in him becoming lighter on his forehand, which is essential to good jumping.

POSTURE

Keep the correct jumping seat to avoid being floppy. A slack position causes your upper body to become very unstable, making it very easy for your horse to throw you off balance. Adopting the position above will enable you to remain in balance should your horse hesitate or attempt to refuse.

With an upright and supported upper body and a secure leg position, you should be able to fold your upper body down towards your horse's withers by keeping your hip joints supple. When jumping in this posture, the momentum of your horse's bascule will cause you to fold forward almost automatically but tension in your hips will hinder the jump and could result in you being 'left behind' or your horse hollowing his back and dropping his hind legs. This reaction of the horse can be caused by too strong a rein contact that does not yield when jumping an obstacle; you should be able to keep the rein contact elastic with a secure jumping seat. Your elbows should rest against the sides of your body with your shoulders square and your chest lifted. Your head should face between your horse's ears with your jaw relaxed (do not grit your teeth!) – the ability to look where you are going is an important factor!

REIN CONTACT

Remember that your reins are for controlling the horse and assisting his balance, not for you to balance yourself with. They should be long enough to enable you to carry your hands just above your horse's withers and allow you to follow the stretch forward of his neck as he bascules over the jump. The contact should remain constant: the rein should not be made loose or pulled tighter as he jumps. If the reins are pulled too tightly, he may knock

A rider in a balanced jumping seat maintaining an elastic contact with her horse's mouth while allowing him full use of his back and neck. (Photo courtesy Frank Grainger Photography.)

the jump with his hind legs because his movement will have been restricted. You need to hold the reins in softly closed fists with your fingers closed enough not to allow the reins to slide through them. In some circumstances it may be desirable to slip the reins, for instance if you have been left behind over a fence. It is better to slip the reins than pull at the horse with tight reins. You should maintain an elastic feeling with your horse's mouth through your elbow, wrist and fingers to allow him full use of his back and neck.

POSITION FOR TAKE-OFF

When reaching the take-off point, your horse must be allowed to take your hands forwards in the direction of his mouth, maintaining a straight line from your elbow to the bit. Your upper body folds forward from your hips with your chest lowering towards your horse's neck and your arms extending forwards. Your backside remains lightly in contact with the saddle and feels as though it is eased backwards towards the cantle (your hips must remain supple in order for this to happen) and your knees should stay in firm contact with the saddle. Your lower legs must remain securely against your horse's sides and not swing backwards, which would make your whole position insecure and you would be unbalanced and pitch forward on landing. Your weight needs to remain on the balls of your feet with your heels well down.

POSITION FOR LANDING

On landing, keep your upper body forward until you feel your horse's hind legs touch the ground. If jumping drop fences, or into bad ground, you may need to come upright earlier to keep your balance should the horse stumble on landing. The most important thing is to keep your lower leg in position no matter what! Keep your whole leg position secure against the saddle, with flexible joints to absorb the impact. Your upper body should lift upright again quite easily, providing your hips remain supple, as your horse steps under with his hind legs and propels himself away from the obstacle. Your elbows return to your sides and your hands back towards the withers. You should both be balanced and ready to approach the next jump. If you come upright too soon, before your horse's hind legs touch down, it is very likely that he will knock the top pole, as his hindquarters will drop too suddenly and he will hollow his back. If you come upright too late you will probably be pitched forward and bang your nose on your horse's neck.

When jumping, always try to remain balanced. To help maintain this balanced position, many riders find it useful to imagine that they would land standing on the ground if their horse disappeared.

Loose Jumping

Jumping without a rider should be a pleasurable experience for your horse which teaches him how to jump independently and allows you to watch him from the ground and assess his natural jumping technique and attitude toward popping over poles. Some horses love jumping, while others remain unconvinced. Working your horse loose will help you to determine whether you have a potential jumping star or future top dressage candidate, although horses who cannot jump are not necessarily good at dressage and there are many horses who excel in both disciplines.

The exercises which follow can either be done with your horse on a lunge line or totally free. It is essential to have access to a safe, enclosed area. If you are worried that your horse might jump out over the school fence (it can happen!), it is best to keep him on the lunge. Only try loose schooling if you are confident, otherwise get professional help.

Lungeing Over Fences

If you are lungeing your horse over a fence, use a lunge cavesson so that you do not accidentally pull him in the mouth. Your horse should wear brushing boots on all four legs for protection, but do not use side reins, a chambon, or any other gadget, because he must be totally free from restriction in his neck and back in order to balance himself properly.

Start with a single pole on the ground. After lungeing your horse for a few minutes to warm him up, ask him to approach the pole in trot. He should stretch down a little and look at the pole as he goes over it. Repeat this exercise a few times in each direction, establishing a steady rhythm as your horse gains confidence. Next, raise the pole off the ground about 0.3 m (1 ft) by using plastic blocks as supports. It helps to position a pole on the side away from the wall on the approach from both sides as a wing to help your horse stay straight.

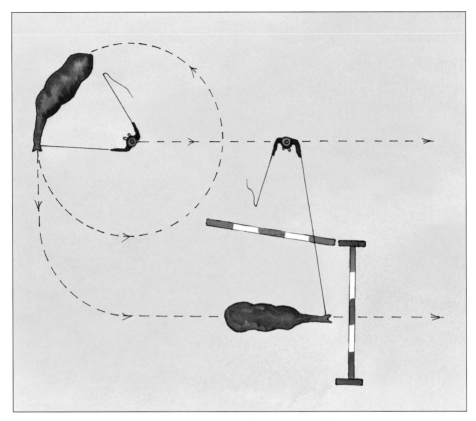

Lunge your horse on a circle at one end of the school. When you approach the jump/pole on the ground, make sure the approach is straight, and you allow him to land straight afterwards. You will have to move up the school with him.

Lunge your horse once or twice on a 15 m circle in trot at one end of the school on the approach side of the jump. The jump needs to be halfway down the long side of the school at right angles to the wall and close to the side. If you leave a gap, you run the risk of the horse trying to run through it. Once you have established a steady trot, move in a straight line down the school, lining your horse up with the centre of the small jump. This is important because he must be able to take off evenly from both hind legs. If you are still on a circle with him, he will not be straight; instead, he will lean in like a motor bike with his weight on his inside legs. You have to move up the school while lungeing your horse so that he approaches the jump straight and lands straight on all four feet. Try not to hook him around with the rein afterwards – it is better to guide him around with small tugs on the line with a relaxed hand. Approach the pole in trot again. Your horse should jump in a calm manner without speeding up. If he fizzes up, bring him away from the jump and lunge him on a circle until he settles down and then try again.

Start with one jump only, as two means a quick sprint up the school!

Once you have mastered this exercise in trot, let your horse canter the last two or three strides. If he canters of his own volition, this is not a problem provided he is calm and not going too fast. If he gets too quick, carefully resume the lunge circle away from the jump until he has settled down again, then repeat the jump in a better rhythm. Make sure that you can bring him quietly back to trot again afterwards. Cantering your horse the whole way on the lunge means that you have to be a good runner and not inclined to trip over your own feet!

While it is best to keep the jump low when lunging over jumps, you can make a small ascending spread, or a parallel, but no more than 0.75 m (2½ ft) high, because you must be able to control your horse. A total of fifteen minutes of jumping in this way is a long session, so aim to finish on time with stretching work to help your horse relax mentally and physically.

Loose Schooling Over Fences

Jumping your horse totally loose requires an indoor school, a very high fence or a walled area, which will stop your horse from jumping out. It is possible to loose-jump your horse on your own, but a willing assistant means less running around allied with easier and safer initial sessions. It is preferable for people to be fairly experienced with lungeing before they try loose schooling.

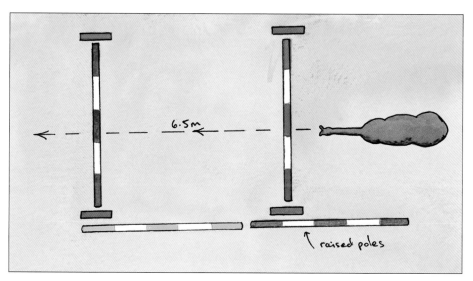

A simple double made into a jumping lane with raised poles alongside, high enough to prevent the horse jumping out.

To start, build a jumping lane. Set up blocks as supports for two small jumps one non-jumping stride apart (about 6.5 m or 21 ft). Place a pole on the ground by the first set of supports, then make a small, ascending spread jump (0.5 m or1½ ft) by the second set of supports. Enclose the obstacles with a line of three raised poles, which are high enough to prevent the horse jumping out (one before, sloping up to the first fence; one beside, high enough to prevent him nipping out between the two obstacles; and one after, sloping away from the second fence). Build it close against one wall of the school so that your horse cannot accidentally come up on the outside.

Have a small bucket of food tucked away in a safe place as a reward for your horse. Send him around the school. If you have a helper, each of you needs a lunge whip. If you are on you own, stay in line with your horse's belly at all times. If you get ahead of him he will turn around and go off in the other direction. He should approach the jumping lane in a steady trot and will probably canter the last couple of strides of his own volition. Once he is steadily cantering (ideally, he will settle in to his own rhythm), keep him going by pointing the whip towards his hocks and move up the school yourself keeping in line with his belly to help him approach in a straight line. Avoid chasing your horse with the whip. Once he has completed three or four attempts well, halt him with your voice and reward him for his hard work. Your horse will then learn that when you stop him he gets a reward. This develops his trust in you and should prevent him from tearing around like a lunatic.

Change the jump and pole around the other way and repeat the exercise.

An experienced showjumper enjoying his loose jumping. An ascending spread encourages the horse to lift through his forehand.

The whole training session should take fifteen to twenty minutes and will probably be quite tiring for you both. The pole can be raised to make a jump, so that in future sessions you have a small double, with the first jump being a simple upright and the second a small inviting spread.

A short session of loose jumping once a week or every ten days will benefit your training programme and increase your and your horse's enjoyment of the process. Remember that these exercises should be fun for your horse and help him to become agile and confident in his own abilities.

Virtual Jumping

Using 'virtual jumps' will help you to develop a good jumping technique, particularly your approach to related fences, judging distances between fences and varying the gait, and building confidence in you and your horse without worrying about the height of the fences. Virtual jumping is also an excellent way of getting back into jumping after a break and of introducing a young horse to obstacles.

The Virtual Course

To start, set out a jumping course of about eight obstacles using poles on the ground. Be imaginative and include a mini-parallel of two poles 0.5 m (1½ ft) apart, so that your horse can see and step over both poles. If they are further apart than this, he will not be sure whether to jump over them or step between them, which is why trotting poles should always incorporate either one pole or three and over, not two on their own.

Ride in the saddle you will be jumping in with your stirrups adjusted to jumping length, which should be at least two or three holes shorter than dressage length for most people. Remember that it can be disconcerting for your horse if one minute you have long stirrups and the next minute you shorten them up. It is better to plan a jumping session which begins with your stirrups the shorter length. This way, your horse will get used to where your legs are and learn to associate this length of leg for jumping and a longer leg for dressage. This also gets you used to riding (and finding your balance) in your jumping seat and starts to work muscles which are not used in the same way in dressage training.

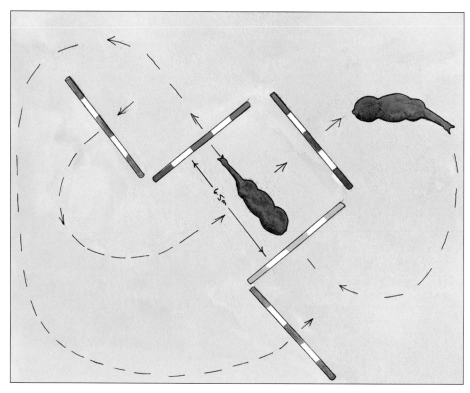

A sample of a virtual jumping course allowing various options, including a one-stride double set at 6.5 m (21 ft).

Place the virtual jumps so that you can ride them all from both directions, which means that you do not have to interrupt your training session to get off and move them around.

WALKING OVER THE VIRTUAL JUMPS

Plan the course route in your head and walk your horse over the poles. While you are doing this, think about your approach to each jump and aim straight at the middle of each pole. (A different, more advanced exercise for another schooling session is to practise approaching at an angle. It is easy to experiment like this without risking refusals or knockdowns if you get it wrong.) More importantly, think about the pattern that you are riding on the ground. Each turn should be an even loop, or part of a circle. Keep the rhythm and tempo of the walk the same all through your course, while you turn your shoulders toward each jump. You should continue until you both feel confident and calm. This exercise is a good one for instructors to use when teaching novice pupils the importance of accurate flatwork when jumping. Many novice riders assume that they do not need to steer when they are jumping – they think that the horse will automatically take them to the jumps. How wrong they are!

As you proceed, concentrate on sitting up straight in the saddle, exactly as you would for dressage schooling. Practise half-halts, remembering to close your knees as necessary while keeping a steady lower leg. Give your leg aids without your lower leg swinging back so that you practise your jumping position between the jumps. When you have completed the approach to each pole, look ahead to the next jump to help you focus on it.

Give your horse correct turning aids with your body – do not forget your basic school movements just because you are training for jumping. Sit on your inside seat bone and keep your weight on your inside stirrup, without leaning in. This weight aid into the stirrup is necessary to make a good turn into a jump. If you lean in you will unbalance your horse.

Walking the course establishes confidence and calmness before progressing to trot or canter.

PROGRESSING TO TROT AND CANTER
Proceed to rising trot and ride your course in an even rhythm, letting your horse think for himself about picking his feet up over the poles. Jumping horses must be encouraged to think for themselves, because it is an intrinsi-

cally good idea that they do so and because they should be able to get you out of trouble if you make a mistake. Horses who are too reliant on their riders will not be able to help if left to their own devices, which can result in nasty falls. When jumping, your job is to ride a good approach in a steady rhythm. Once you reach take-off point, a horse that has been encouraged to develop self-confidence will usually sort himself out. However, a rider who has established a partnership with the horse and is aware of the horse's preferred technique, will be able to act as a partner rather than a passenger at the point of take-off.

You should concentrate on riding the stride, not the fence. If you have everything else right, such as balance and straightness, your horse will know when to take off. This will become apparent as you ride your virtual course in canter. Establish a good working canter and practise keeping this same canter throughout the course. Move into your jumping (light) seat and stay there round the course to establish your lower leg position. Then progress to sitting upright, or slightly in front of the vertical between the poles, and coming forward with your upper body as you feel your horse lift himself up over each pole. He will give you a small spring over each pole, helping you to feel when he takes off so that you do not get left behind or pitch forward.

Practise keeping the canter balanced on the turns, making appropriate changes of canter lead as you go; change through trot, then walk. The poles give you the chance to get this right without the risk of spoiling the approach to a bigger jump because the jumps are so small. Keep your horse in a soft, low outline which helps him to round his back and use his neck to balance correctly. If he is listening to your aids you should ride a smooth course, including lining up each approach well and riding forward to the next jump. Riding your horse forward does not mean speeding up – it is about thinking forward with him 'in front of your leg', i.e. responsive to a light leg aid.

Finish your virtual jumping session by returning to rising trot around the course, popping over the occasional pole as you go. Move into walk and encourage your horse to stretch long and low to release his muscles and encourage him to relax mentally. The session should be between thirty and forty minutes long, depending on how fit you both are!

Take-off and Landing

Take-off

Great jumping does not happen by accident – it is the result of regular training and a positive bond between horse and rider. You need to give your horse the best chance possible to make a good jump over an obstacle. Your objective is to present him to the fence straight, in a good rhythm and with enough weight on his hocks to propel himself into the air, much like a jumbo jet with the engines revved up for sufficient take-off thrust.

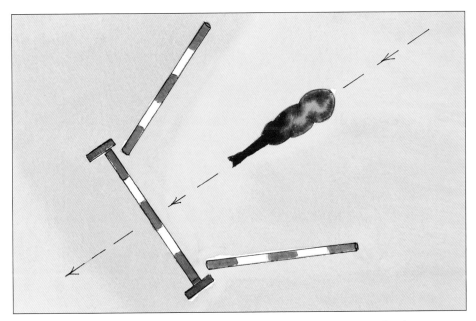

Two poles at an angle to help a straight take-off in the centre of the fence.

Place two poles at an angle with one either side of the approach side of a jump, with the narrow end nearest the jump, and the widest further away. As you approach the jump, the V shape acts as a tunnel to ride between to help you practise a straight approach.

Next, set the poles out as random jumps. Lay two poles out as a double approximately 6.5 m (21 ft) apart, or six and a half human strides. This allows room to land, take one non-jumping stride and take off again in-between the poles. Practice striding out the correct distances yourself and you will get it right every time. For two non-jumping strides, the distance should be about 10.5 m (34½ ft) or ten and a half human strides.

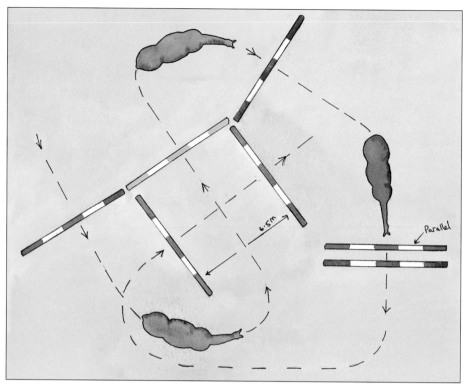

6.5 m

Parallel

A small course including a parallel and a one-stride double. The double should be set at approximately 6.5 m (21½ ft) allowing for landing, one non-jumping canter stride and taking off again.

Ride this small course in an energetic working trot, which means having impulsion, not going fast. You should not need to alter the distance between the poles of the double. The horse should take about five trot strides in total between the poles; one counting as landing and one as taking off again. The non-jumping canter stride will equal about three trot steps. Your horse will not jump the poles at this stage, but he might hop over them. Keep him in a soft outline with his neck fairly low to encourage him to round his back and pick up his feet. If he trips, then he is on his forehand and his hind legs are not engaged. If this happens, spend a few minutes working around the poles using frequent transitions and half-halts to put some spring into his step and to improve his balance.

Starting with the single poles, line yourselves up with the middle of each pole on the approach without altering the rhythm or length of the stride. Look straight ahead to the space beyond the pole, which encourages your horse to do the same and to move forward towards the next obstacle. If you look down at the pole, he will too and he might stop. If you feel your horse hesitate, quickly give a firm leg aid, perhaps followed by a tap with the whip. Stay calm and approach consecutive poles as though nothing has happened. If you hit a problem, wipe it from your memory and start afresh with the next approach. The aim of these exercises is cumulative success.

Progress to a bouncy working canter in a round outline while you keep an elastic contact with the reins. The canter stride over each pole will feel slightly elevated during pole work and your horse might treat each pole as a small jump if you have him correctly on his hocks. If he does, then let him take your upper body slightly forward; follow the stretch of his neck with your hands. There is no need to drop the contact, but it is better to give with your reins rather than to hang on to your horse's mouth and prevent him from stretching forward. Look at each pole and line yourself up for a straight approach, then look ahead to the next one. Your horse will know when to pick his feet up if you present him to the pole straight and in balance. There is no need to count strides at this stage, because it is much better to get the feeling of your horse taking off. If you make a mistake counting the strides you will either have a refusal or a poor jump, so leave it to your horse to get you out of trouble! Approach the pole in a slightly

Taking off over a 'virtual' jump. Provided the horse has his hind legs underneath his body, his forehand will lift!

forward position with your backside in the saddle, so that you can really feel what your horse is doing. Concentrate on riding the stride, i.e. keeping a regular rhythm in a balanced canter rather than riding at the pole like a demon! As your horse lifts himself off the ground, let him take the reins and your hands forward, bend from your hips, and point your backside towards the back of the saddle. This will keep your weight over your knees and you in balance with your horse. The basic principles are the same whether the obstacle is a pole on the ground or a six-foot high wall. The rider's aim is to keep in balance with the horse, and this means adapting your posture with reference to the actual physical changes undergone by the horse. For example, during ascent over a high obstacle, the horse's body will be angled upward more steeply than if he is jumping a low spread. Therefore, in order to keep in balance with the horse, the rider's upper body will need to be angled more forward when jumping a big upright than when jumping a low spread.

Landing

Remain quietly in balance in the air. As your horse puts his front feet on the ground, close your knees against the saddle to brace your thighs, with your joints acting as shock absorbers cushioning your upper body. Stay forward with your shoulders until you feel your horse's back legs touch the ground. The momentum of his hindquarters coming underneath him will bring your upper body upright again. Unfortunately, if you are tight in your hips you will pitch forward. Keep your weight even in your stirrups to balance yourself and the horse. You will not be in a good position to approach the next pole if you lean to one side. Bring your hands back to their normal position by your horse's withers and keep him into the bridle with your legs. Ride away from the pole to make a fresh approach to the next one. Avoid leaning on your horse's neck with your hands, which spoils your rein contact and leaves your horse hollowing his back and neck on landing. This might seem insignificant over a pole, but it will put him very much on his forehand over a big jump. Your weight will be too far forward and you could end up banging your nose on his neck!

When riding a double, or a series of obstacles, you must react quickly between landing and taking off again. If you remain in a forward seat all the time, you will get more forward over each pole and end up unable to

Landing in balance sets up a good approach to the next obstacle.

come upright again. As you land over the first pole, bring your upper body into the approach position, keeping your horse on his hocks ready for the next take-off. Remember to rebalance the canter with a half-halt on the non-jumping stride or strides.

Turns Into Jumps: The Approach

Turning toward jumps or poles is no different from riding any other turn across the school, when riding across country or when out hacking and hanging a sharp left or right. Do not let your basic schoolwork go out of the window just because there are poles on the ground or jumps in the way. No matter what you want to do with your horse, you will need to be able to execute quick and accurate turns.

Working on a Circle

Begin by setting the poles out in a large star shape. The ends of the poles should be about 10 m (33 ft) apart across the centre of the star. Ride a big

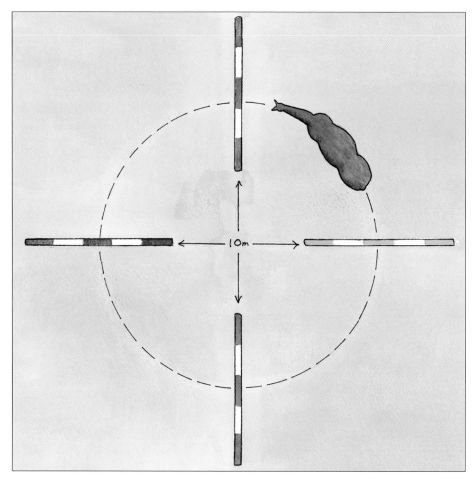

Concentrate on lining yourself up with the centre of each pole.

circle in working trot, lining your horse up so that you go straight over the centre point of each pole. Because you are on a big circle your body should be positioned for the appropriate bend: keep your upper body tall with your weight in your inside stirrup. Try not to overdo this and lean in because your horse will cut in, lean on his inside shoulder and hang on your inside rein for support. Repeat on the other rein. Concentrate on keeping the rhythm of the stride regular and aim to take the same number of steps between each pole, so you do not alter the length of stride between the poles. Collect or lengthen your horse's stride to fit easily around the four poles. Once you have achieved this, his confidence will grow and he will become more relaxed through his back. Practise this exercise in a light seat to establish your jumping position.

Then, take two poles away, leaving one on either side of the circle. Proceed to canter. Establish a light seat again, keeping your balance as you turn around the circle. This will help your horse's balance and encourage him to look after himself when you are out of the saddle. Also, by cantering in a light seat you will not restrict your horse's back movement. You must develop a secure lower leg position to keep your weight correctly into your inside stirrup. Your outside leg needs to stay down and back to maintain the canter lead and to stop your horse from changing leg.

Make sure that you are not leaning on your horse's neck for balance; maintain an elastic contact to keep him in a low, round outline and encourage him to use his lumbar muscles.

Ride one half circle out of the saddle in canter and the other half circle sitting with your upper body slightly forward. This will help you to become adept at changing your upper body position. If you are more upright, you will be able to set your horse up for a turn. If you are more forward, he will be able to lift off the ground when he jumps. The rhythm and length of the canter stride should not alter whether you are in the saddle or out of it. To achieve this, you need a supple back and flexible hips. If you want to steady the stride, use half-halts to set your horse more on his hocks and a firmer outside rein to control his outside shoulder but do not overdo it or you will lose the correct bend.

Establish a balanced trot and focus on your line of attack before attempting the approach in canter.

To practice turning more acutely – which is useful if you need extra corner-cutting in a jump off, or more manoeuvrability when hacking through woods for example – make the circle smaller by riding continuous balanced turns at the inner edge of the poles. Ride one or two circles like this before spiralling out to a big circle around the poles to give your horse a break and to help his inside hind leg come more under his body. This also guards against motor-biking around the circle. To check that your horse will still move away from your inside leg, keep your outside rein as a support for your horse's shoulders. Maintain enough bend around your inside leg to ensure control over the size and shape of the circle. Look around the circle to the next pole to give yourself time to plan the next half circle.

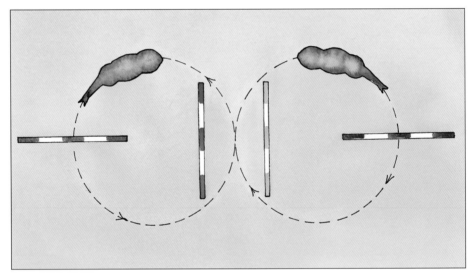

A figure-of-eight with a pole at each side, and two parallel poles in the centre.

Figures-of-eight

Progress to a figure-of-eight, cantering over a pole at each end and between two parallel ones in the middle. In the beginning, keep the figure-of-eight big by using the whole schooling area. As you get better at turning, make it smaller so that the turns become tighter. Make a transition to trot as you pass between the poles at the centre, giving yourself a few steps to change your horse's bend and to set him up for the new direction. At a later stage, make the transition to walk to help collect the canter, giving more bounce and lift to the stride. As with the earlier exercise, keep an even number of strides; there should not be a difference if you are riding the same shape and size of circle at each end of the figure-of-eight. The central poles will keep you from drifting either way as you change your bend, and a flying change can be added at this point later on (see pages 179–180). If you can keep a regular rhythm in the canter then adjust the route around the circle to have the same number of steps in both circles. This is better than messing around with your horse's natural rhythm, because you do not want to spoil his canter. His stride will become very jerky and irregular if you continually hook him back and then send him sharply forward as you get to the pole. Again, ride the stride, not the pole!

Finish by cantering around the arena, gradually lengthening the reins so that your horse stretches down and relaxes. Stay in a light seat. Your horse should stay balanced if your canter work has been correct.

Jumping Straight

If you are going to jump anything successfully, you and your horse must be able to jump straight. If you are show jumping, straightness is essential when tackling combinations of jumps in a sequence, because if you veer one way or the other, you will end up shooting past the last element or you could crash into a wing and injure yourself. If you are going across country, you need to set your horse straight at the jumps to ensure that you can jump cleanly and safely. Many cross-country courses include arrowheads, zigzags, etc., so they are worth practising. Even popping over logs and other natural obstacles while out hacking or hunting is easier, safer and more enjoyable when you and your horse are straight.

If your horse becomes tense during the following exercises, spend a few minutes working on transitions and leg-yielding exercises to re-establish freedom of movement through his joints. A tight horse will jar himself; the same applies to a tense rider.

Raising Alternate Poles at One End

Before beginning these exercises, set up a line of three poles at trot stride (approximately 1.3 m or 4 ft) apart. Raise alternate poles at one end to help you aim at the centre of the poles. If your horse tends to swerve more one way than the other, you can raise that side of the poles slightly more – so if he falls to the left, raise the left-hand ends of the poles slightly more than the right. Crooked jumping is often related to basic crookedness; the straighter the horse becomes in his flatwork, the more likely he will be to jump straight. However, this is only useful if you are sure that it is not you who is doing the veering, because raising poles more on one side is not a substitute for you not riding your horse straight!

It is important to warm up and establish a regular rhythm in trot before you begin. Adopt and stay in the jumping (light) seat, which will help your horse to pick up his feet more easily as the centre of the poles will be slightly above the ground.

Approach the poles in working trot. Concentrate on keeping yourself evenly balanced and with an even weight in your stirrups. Keep an elastic contact throughout the exercise and your horse stretching through his back in a round outline to help him stay relaxed.

Make sure that you ride extremely straight and maintain your rein and leg aids on both sides. Perform this exercise on both reins, not just your horse's favourite side, otherwise you will not become straighter. Aim to ride

A pole followed by a small jump with two poles in a wide V shape to help a straight approach.

over the middle of each pole, regardless of whichever side is raised. This lessens the risk of your horse running out at the side. If he speeds up and tries it on, approach at a slower, more collected trot, using frequent half-halts to regulate his speed.

This exercise can also be done over poles in a star formation to prevent falling in or out. Raise either the inside edge of the poles more to keep your horse out or the outside edge to keep him from drifting away. A straight horse is easy to turn on a circle, as his hind legs follow the track of his front legs. Again, always aim for the middle of each pole.

When practising riding in a straight line in canter, remember that your leg position needs to maintain the canter lead, with your outside leg stretched down and back to prevent your horse changing legs of his own accord (this outside leg must not be overdone, since too strong an aid may push the quarters out of alignment) and your inside leg at the girth to maintain impulsion. Set two small jumps (leave the first as a pole on the ground to start with) at about 6.5 m (21 ft) apart. This distance allows for landing, one non-jumping stride, and taking off again. Place two additional poles which form a tunnel before the first pole; this should help you to keep straight.

The two approach poles will focus you both towards the centre of the first pole and draw you to the mid-line of the small jump. It is up to you to keep this line as you go over the jump. Maintain the canter and keep an even rhythm, which should prevent your horse from hollowing his back and help him to maintain a correct outline. Look up and ahead to the space beyond the small jump to focus you both forward and to keep a consistent speed. Try to look at where you are going next and continue to ride straight after the jump to give yourself time to make a downward transition with your horse remaining straight. This will teach him not to run off around the corner in between poles or jumps and keep him listening to you.

An additional jump can be added (about 6.5 m or 21 ft away) once you are proficient at this. Also, up to three or four canter poles can be added on the approach to increase the difficulty of this exercise. Aim to keep your horse absolutely straight throughout the line of small jumps and poles.

After riding this exercise a few times, go large and practise riding straight lines and turns without going over any poles. After you turn, prepare to go straight and to turn away from a straight line in good time for your next turn. This is easy to do if you go straight up the sides and ride even turns through each corner.

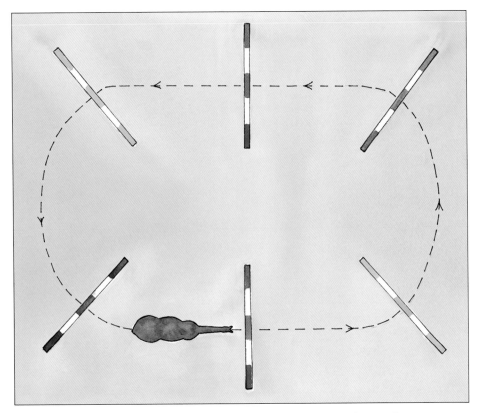

Poles laid around the school in the corners and one on each long side.

Using Side and Corner Poles

Another exercise involves placing a pole in the middle of each long side, and one in each corner at an angle, to help you ride each corner in the same way. This can be done in trot and then canter as the poles are well spaced out around the school. Aim straight at the poles on the long sides. Prepare for each corner and remember to turn your shoulders so that they are level with the corner poles. Your horse should be correctly bent around your inside leg, so that you can straighten him up again with your body by straightening yourself up. Do not rely on the reins to bring his neck straight; instead, concentrate on bringing his shoulders into line with his hind legs with your shoulders, inside leg and outside rein. This is a good exercise to finish off this training session as it can be done in walk, trot or canter on a long rein.

Impulsion: Maintaining Power

Confusing impulsion with speed is a common mistake.

Impulsion is the power emanating from a horse who is using his hocks correctly and bringing his haunches under him. The result is an outline with an uphill appearance and a horse who gives the impression that he wants to move forward and is listening and responsive to the rider's legs. A horse with real impulsion will be well muscled and look as though he has been body building! Impulsion is essential for dressage, show jumping and cross-country – a horse working with good impulsion can spring a lot higher than one who is not.

Speed is simply going faster – a horse can be on his forehand, heavy on the reins with his hocks trailing behind, and still gain momentum, while he is simultaneously out of balance and tight through his back. A horse using his impulsion correctly to travel at speed will remain light, well balanced and straight.

The following exercises will help you and your horse to gain impulsion.

Using cavalletti to generate impulsion to improve straightness. Riding between two parallel poles helps to check the straightness.

Pole Work at Canter

To start, set the poles out at a canter stride (approximately 3.5 m or 11½ ft) apart, so that your horse has to bounce over each pole in succession. Begin with three poles in a row, as most horses will easily cope with this. This exercise can be made more difficult by increasing the number of poles; to progress, add one extra pole at a time. If you are using a long sequence of poles, it may be a good idea to set them up across the diagonal of the school (provided that turns to and from the diagonal can be ridden correctly at canter). This gymnastic work is excellent for building your horse's muscle tone, but be sure not to work for long periods without a break or a stretch. Ten to fifteen minutes is enough for any of these exercises.

By keeping the energy (impulsion) in the canter, whether it is collected, working or medium, your horse should have enough spring to arrive at the last pole of the planned sequence. This is how you can judge how many poles you should use for these exercises. As you approach, assess whether or not you have enough power to get over the last pole in the line, not the first. If you do not, abandon your approach and turn smoothly away in time, not sharply at the last moment. These variations in the gait will affect striding between the poles, so you will need to adjust the distances accordingly. Work on the quality of the canter for a few more minutes, then try again. You should still be in the light forward seat for this. Rest if your legs are getting tired, as this will spoil your concentration. It is important to stop pole work before you or your horse get too tired, because this is when accidents happen.

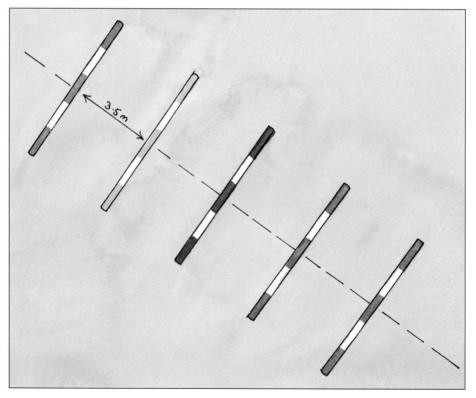

A line of poles set at 3.5 m (11½ ft), which allows the horse to canter over each pole without a non-jumping stride.

Establish a bouncy canter, somewhere between a collected canter and a working canter. To achieve this, use transitions from walk to canter and canter to trot or walk if your horse is balanced enough and really on his hocks, and direct transitions from canter to halt. Your horse must be using his hind legs properly before you start. Once you have the canter, approach the line of poles, maintaining the rhythm and stride. By starting with three poles, you can check that you have the distance correct for your horse. If they are too wide, he will be putting in irregular strides here and there. If they are too close, you run the risk of him leaping over two at once. Stay in a light seat so you do not disturb your horse and can follow his movement easily, even if he makes the odd mistake (or bucks out of exuberance). Maintain your horse's outline, but keep a light contact so that he can still use his neck to stretch forward and to balance himself. Be accommodating while aware of the important things like building his confidence and keeping the energy (impulsion) as you go. After the poles, keep the same canter around your schooling area and then try the poles again a few times in succession so that he gets the idea of flowing forward.

After a rest, return to canter and work on transitions within the canter. Think of these as powerful gear changes from first to fourth gear, rather than going faster or slower. The canter should get bigger as you go up a gear, and more bouncy in a lower gear. Both the bigger medium canter and the springy collected canter require a lot of impulsion. The collected canter has the effect of bouncing the horse like a spring, and the medium canter releases the spring so that the canter bounds forward.

With the poles at a slightly shorter distance apart to accommodate a collected stride, bounce your horse along the line of poles. After going over the poles, go up into working canter around the school, then to medium canter, to feel the difference between them. If your horse can collect and lengthen properly, it will also be vastly easier for him to adjust his stride on the approach. This has a lot of benefits when jumping courses. If you feel out of control, then your horse is no longer using his hind legs correctly – he is falling on to his forehand and pulling. Test your horse's balance frequently by making a direct transition from canter to walk or halt, *depending on his level of training*.

Next, space the poles out to approximately 4 m (13 ft) apart so that you can ride a bigger canter, which should be between working and medium canter. Your horse will take bigger strides over these poles but should be in balance at the end, allowing you to bring him back to a collected canter, then make a transition either to trot or walk to keep him balanced.

Introducing a Small Course of Jumps

The pole work that you have done so far should have set an excellent foundation for you and your horse to successfully cope with a course of small jumps. After developing your horse's jumping technique and your position safely over poles, you should now be ready to tackle jumps.

Trotting Poles

First, warm up and practise over trotting poles to get you both limbered up and in the right frame of mind, then set four poles in a square. The distance between the poles should be approximately 6.5 m (21 ft), allowing for landing, one non-jumping stride, and taking off again for an average horse. If you have a smaller pony the distance will be slightly less, while a big horse with a bigger stride will need a distance of about 7 m (23 ft). Set the jump wings or blocks out first, so that the poles can be raised into jumps later, and place the poles on the ground where the jumps will be.

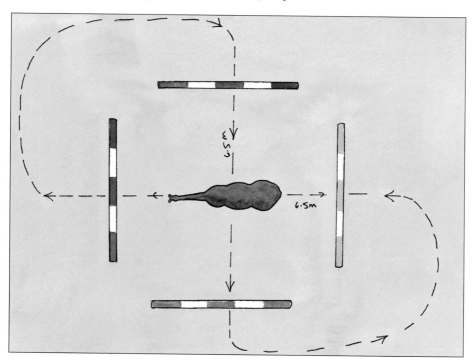

Poles set in a square creating two doubles, each allowing one non-jumping stride between the elements.

Trot over one double of poles in rising trot, then turn toward the other double. Keep a nice flowing rhythm in your trot over the poles in a figure-of-eight pattern three or four times in succession, so that you get used to linking jumps together in a sequence. You might need a single small jump at one end of the school as a confidence booster to pop over now and again. An average jumping course consists of between eight to ten jumps, so you need to build up to jumping this many in one go. Remember to keep breathing and try to maintain your horse's outline without restricting him. These exercises should be fun for both of you!

Progressing to Jumps

Next, raise the second pole of each double off the ground about 0.3 m (1 ft). Ride the sequence in trot again to get the feeling for when your horse will take off. Remember to ride the trot and not the jump by letting the jump come to you. Have a rest in between the exercises and, to prevent accidents, stop before you both get too tired.

Raise the front poles as well for the next session, so you have two small doubles of about 0.75 m (2½ ft) in height. Establish a good working canter by going over your single practice jump a couple of times in each direction. Make sure that your turns are accurate and your changes of leg – through trot or walk – are good quality. You do not want to unbalance your horse. (Flying changes are dealt with on pages 179–180.) Line yourself up for one of the doubles and maintain your canter towards it. Make sure that you have enough impulsion to get over the second element and away to the next double. Trust your horse to pick his feet up at the right moment and, most importantly, do not panic just because there is a jump in front of you! As you take off, maintain the gait with your lower legs. If you have a good approach at the right speed, there is no need to give an extra-strong aid on take-off, this should be for emergencies only. If you do this at the wrong moment, the horse may well make a mistake. If the horse stumbles between elements, or makes a mistake, keep your legs on, and maintain your position and balance. You may need to slip the reins to allow him to regain his balance. The horse will recover better if you sit quietly than if you take evasive action! Change your canter lead after the first jump and head straight for the next double. Continue doing this until you have done eight jumps, or four doubles. Have a rest and let your horse have a good stretch on a long rein. While you are walking around your schooling area, think about how you and your horse tackled these jumps. If you both coped well, raise one double to about 1m (3 ft). Jump the lower one again, followed by the higher one. If your position is correct and you have the right rhythm and impulsion you will be pleased to discover that there is no difference in the technique needed for either double.

Make sure that your hips remain supple so that your horse can move you into a forward position in the air. Keep your upper body down until you feel his hind legs touch the ground. Soften the reins as he jumps, bringing them back into an elastic contact as you land so you are ready to ride him into a good turn toward the next double. You are now reaping the benefits of all that you have been practising!

Once you are happy with the square of doubles, add in extra small jumps and a small ascending spread and a narrow parallel around the arena to give you and your horse more variety. You should enjoy these jumps if your previous pole work has been good.

Shows

When you are jumping confidently at home, you are ready for your first outing to a small show.

Enter a low-key local show to help you and your horse get used to the atmosphere. Try to remember that the most unnerving part is the warm-up arena where you will encounter many horses and riders who tend to speed around big jumps and who are completely oblivious to other people trying to work in. Leave them to it and ride exactly as you have been doing at home, establishing your canter, transitions and turns. Have a warm-up plan worked out which reflects a condensed version of exactly how you would school your horse at home.

You will only need a couple of small practice jumps to get into gear; the most important thing is to keep calm and maintain the rhythm. You might have to be a bit firmer with your aids and keep a more solid position to reassure your horse if he gets a bit excited by the atmosphere, but if you keep your mind positively on the job in hand, your horse will concentrate, too.

Enter for two classes, which are well within your capabilities. If you are jumping less than 1m (3 ft) high at home, enter novice level classes; it is important that your first outing is happy and successful for you both. If you overface yourself and your horse at your first show, it could take months to get your confidence and performance level back again. This also applies to the practice arena. How often do you see people 'practising refusals' at a badly-sited practice fence which is 0.5 m (1½ ft) higher than anything in their actual class. If you and your horse have done well during your first few outings, progress through the levels of class as you gain in technique and confidence. If you want to take jumping seriously, aim to affiliate you both. Affiliation means registering both yourself and your horse with the British Show Jumping Association (USA Equestrian). Structured competitions with set regulations are held for all levels of ability over safe, attractive courses built by registered course builders. Building up your jumping technique in this way ensures that if you are going to compete seriously, you should have no problem coping.

Jumping should be fun, whatever level you are aiming for. Dressage horses benefit enormously from jumping to give them variety in their work and as gymnastic training. Similarly, show jumpers benefit from dressage to establish all the basics and maintain suppleness and balance.

A solid show-jumping technique is essential for eventing or any kind of

Introducing small jumps helps to build the confidence of both horse and rider preparing them to tackle higher obstacles at a later stage.

cross-country riding, even popping over the occasional log while out hacking.

Introducing Cross-country-style Jumps

Jumping cross-country should be great fun for you and your horse. Going across country tests all of your riding skills, especially if you decide to take up eventing, which involves a dressage test, a show-jumping course and a cross-country course. If you are thinking of eventing, you need to be as fit as your horse, because your muscles will quickly tire if you lack stamina – maintaining your position over a course of even fifteen to twenty jumps at the lower levels is hard work! Cross-country jumps involve a variety of different obstacles and you must practise them safely before tackling them in a competition.

Poles set out as a V showing a good example of virtual jumping: a virtual arrowhead.

Simulating Cross-country Fences

In your schooling area, first set out poles as mock cross-country jumps. Include a small parallel, with two parallel poles about 0.8 m apart. A corner, or a narrower version, sometimes known as an arrowhead, is a feature of most courses. For this, place two poles in a narrow V shape, making a small spread with one end narrow and one wide. When jumping it, aim for the middle, so when you set it out make sure it is not more that 0.8 m (2½ ft) wide in the middle for your first few attempts.

Set out two parallel poles to simulate a ditch and place a piece of blue plastic, anchored down by the poles, in between. Place a pole on either side of the ditch, about 6.5 m (21 ft) away, allowing for landing, one non-jumping stride, and taking off again. This simulates a coffin jump, i.e. a ditch with a jump either side.

Place three poles as a zigzag jump, so that you can jump over either end or over the middle.

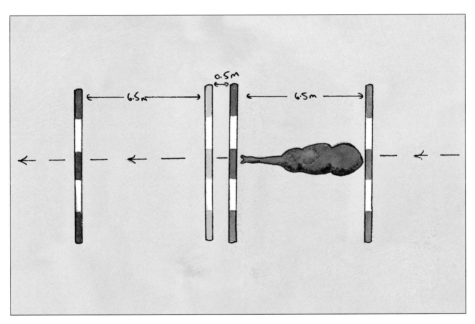

An example of a coffin jump with the space between the elements set at 6.5 m (21 ft). A piece of blue plastic can be added between the poles to simulate water.

Establish a working canter in your jumping seat; get a good rhythm going and make sure that your horse has enough impulsion (not speed) to jump the various spread jumps. Jump a simple upright to get yourself going

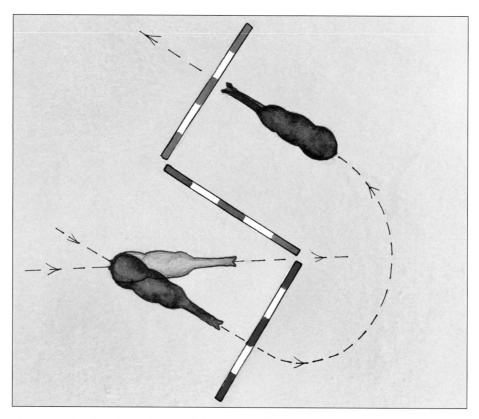

An example of a zigzag jump with optional lines of approach.

and then move on to the parallel poles. Keep the canter flowing to the poles and your horse should jump them easily. This will give you the feeling of how much more he stretches out though his shoulders and pushes off his hocks. Be ready to soften your reins so that your horse can stretch his neck. This is important once you get out on to undulating ground, where your horse will need to use his neck like a balancing pole.

Next, try the corner with the same canter and position. Aim straight for the middle and look ahead to the space in front of you to encourage your horse to keep moving forward. This is no different from riding a parallel, but it is more off-putting for most riders as it looks very wide at one end. Focus on keeping calm and remaining relaxed, even though it looks different. Canter away from the poles in a determined manner to get ready for the next obstacle.

Try the coffin. Be aware that your horse might shy at the blue plastic. To be on the safe side, approach the combination in a positive trot, because it is much harder for your horse to refuse in trot, as he only has one hind leg on the ground at a time and so cannot plant himself. In canter, his hind legs are closer together in the canter sequence, so he can easily put the brakes on if he feels like it! So trot on in a calm, determined manner, looking ahead to the space beyond the third element. You need enough impulsion to get you over all three parts without running out of steam. Have the attitude that you are going over it no matter what. Do not look down, especially when jumping real ditches, otherwise you will probably end up sitting in them.

Once you are happy with these ground-pole obstacles, raise them off the ground. The V and the parallel need to be raised level both ends, otherwise they can look very confusing. With the coffin, raise the third element after the ditch, so that you both focus on it. Once you are happy with this, then the first element can also be raised off the ground. When you are tackling these obstacles confidently, you can venture on to a cross-country course.

Cross-country Courses

Many people like to choose a low cross-country course that they can hire with a friend or group of people from their yard or barn. It might be worth finding out if there is a UK Chasers course near you; these consist of a designated cross-country ride with optional obstacles on route. It is a good idea to take someone with you as a confidence boost and in case anything untoward happens. Use appropriate boots on your horse's legs and wear a body protector when going across country. Now is a good time to check your hat. If it is more than a few years old, or if you have had a fall in it, it is a good idea to buy a new hat which meets the BHS (ASTM/SEI) and international standards.

Pick simple logs and small ditches to start with, repeating the exercises that you were doing in the school. This will reassure your horse and boost your confidence. If you start galloping around, he will get confused, worried and completely over-excited – and the next time you take him cross-country he will probably take off with you! Keep your actions calm and controlled, progressing from trot to canter as you gain experience. When you are comfortable and know that the brakes work, you can go up a gear into a stronger canter to tackle the jumps. Do not attempt an obstacle if you are unsure how the horse will react to it, since you must be committed to positive results and building confidence. Therefore, wait until experience convinces you that your horse is ready.

With water jumps, a strong, matter-of-fact trot is best. Try not to let your horse paddle around in the water, because this might encourage him to get down and roll.

Once you and your horse are cruising happily and safely around cross-country courses, you might like to consider entering a small hunter trial. The British Horse Trials Association (United States Eventing Association) will have details of competitions in your area. Once you have sufficient cross-country experience, you could enter a one-day event, which will put all of your training to excellent use!

Part V

Further Dressage Training

Leg-Yield and Shoulder-in

Leg-yield

The leg-yield is a movement in which the horse travels forwards and sideways away from the pressure of one of your legs. It simply teaches him that if you use one leg, he moves away from it. No lateral bending is required, apart from a slight flexion away from the direction of travel. The horse crosses his legs the same amount, both in front and behind, and simply moves forwards and sideways.

Begin in walk. To ride a leg-yield travelling to the right, sit as for a left flexion, i.e. on your left seat bone, left leg by the girth, right leg behind the girth. Keep a slight flexion to the left away from the direction of travel, maintaining a soft inside rein and a supporting outside rein. Your upper body remains straight to keep the horse straight through his body. Move him sideways with your inside (left) leg nudging him near the girth. It is especially important to keep the inside leg near the girth when leg-yielding in canter, otherwise you risk the horse changing leg. Reverse these aids for a leg-yield to the left.

Shoulder-in

Shoulder-in is the most important lateral movement to master. It is the basis of all the other lateral movements. Shoulder-in is a lateral exercise in which the horse, bent throughout his body around the rider's inside leg, moves forward with his body at an angle of about thirty degrees to the direction of movement. The shoulder-in develops collection in the horse, teaching him to take more weight on his haunches.

Establish this exercise in walk before progressing to trot. This gives you time to feel what the horse is doing and helps you to develop an understanding of how he moves. To ride a shoulder-in to the left, the horse is bent as for a 10 m circle (approximately). This bend is maintained by your position, i.e. your upper body is angled to the left, so that his shoulders are 'in', i.e. off the track or line of travel. Maintain your body

165

position but try to remain supple through your lower back and hip joints to allow the horse to continue in a rhythmic walk. Blocking the movement of the walk causes it to become stilted. Sit on your left seat bone (remaining tall through your upper body), with your left leg near the girth. Flexion to the left is asked for with your inside rein (without pulling). Your outside rein supports the horse's outside shoulder and maintains the angle of the movement in conjunction with your outside knee and thigh, and your lower leg keeps his outside hind leg stepping forward under his body, preventing it from escaping to the outside. When you use your inside leg now, the horse has to move sideways. If the horse is positioned correctly, and the aids are applied correctly, the horse will move down the track with his body bent around your inside leg at an angle of approximately thirty degrees to the line of travel. In this position, he will move on three tracks: his outside hind will make one track, his inside hind and outside fore will step along the same (second) track and his inside fore will make the third track. If the horse is correctly balanced, you should be able to give a little on your inside rein without the horse changing his outline or rhythm. Keep your shoulders level to avoid leaning in or out. If you have a correct bend, your horse should have his neck softly arched, and he will carefully place his inside hind leg forward under his body, lowering his left (inside) hip as he does so. Your weight stays down through your inside leg and your hands remain level maintaining a soft, elastic contact.

SHOULDER-FORE

When introducing shoulder-in for the first time, especially with young or relatively stiff horses, it is better to start with the less demanding exercise of shoulder-fore. Shoulder-fore is a shoulder-in performed with less of an angle. As there is less bend through the horse's body, he will not be travelling quite on three tracks. All four legs will be seen from the front, with the tracks of his inside hind and outside fore close together.

PARALLEL-POLE WORK

Poles are very useful as guide-lines to ride between; it is then far easier to understand the feeling of a correct shoulder-in, and to keep a consistent angle along the side. Set the poles in parallel lines at a distance of 1.5 m (5 ft) apart. The poles help to keep the shoulder-in travelling along a straight line and give you a passageway to ride along, making it much easier to judge the angle.

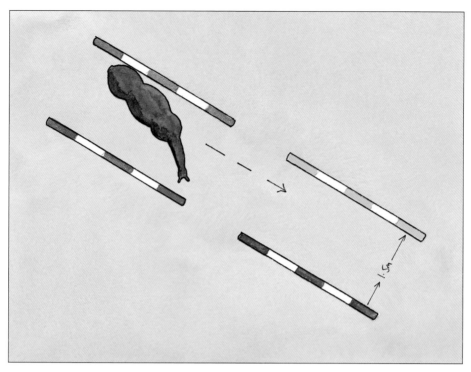

Poles set in parallel lines at 1.5 m (5 ft) apart. The horse is in shoulder-in in relation to the green pole, and shoulder-out in relation to the red one.

SHOULDER-OUT

Shoulder-in is actually shoulder-out in relation to the other line of poles. Both shoulder-out and leg-yield can be ridden facing towards a wall or fence, at an angle of about thirty degrees. In the shoulder-out, the horse is bent as though you are riding a circle towards the wall. From the front three legs would be seen, i.e. the horse moves on three tracks. As already described, in a leg-yield, he simply moves sideways, crossing both fore and hind pairs of legs without a bend through his body, just a flexion away from the line of travel. All four legs would be seen from the front.

MAINTAINING THE CORRECT MOVEMENT

If your horse is on his forehand, he will speed up and wander off in the direction in which he is bent. This needs to be resolved before attempting the exercise again. Use half-halts to maintain the self-carriage of the horse. Make sure that your own position is correct and that you have a good angle with your shoulders to hold the forehand in the correct bend.

If your horse bends his neck more than his body, then you need to check that you are not using too much inside rein. Support him more on the

Shoulder-in to the left. Your outside rein supports the horse's outside shoulder and maintains the angle of the movement in conjunction with your outside leg. Keep the angle of the shoulder-in with your upper body. The yellow pole helps to prevent the outside hind leg from escaping to the outside.

outside of the bend with a firmer contact on your outside rein and by keeping both your legs on more.

A very supple horse may be able to do a shoulder-in on four tracks, while maintaining a correct bend through his body. This is a more advanced movement than a three-track shoulder-in. The angle of your upper body is very important to keeping the angle of your horse's shoulders, and your outside leg must control the outside hind leg of your horse, otherwise the haunches would drift out, losing the bend, turning the movement into a leg-yield. A slightly firmer outside rein and a reduced shoulder angle would reduce the overall angle and give a three-track shoulder-in.

Travers and Renvers

Travers and renvers are valuable suppling exercises, increasing flexibility in the horse's hind leg joints and lumbar region. A degree of collection is established as he lowers his hocks and takes more weight on his hind legs. The exercise is excellent to promote further lateral suppleness of the hindquarters and collection. Renvers is the exact opposite exercise to travers and has the same biomechanical effects.

Riding travers (haunches-in), or its mirror image, renvers (haunches-out) at the correct angle is difficult to feel if you are not familiar with riding these movements. When riding travers, the hindquarters of the horse are brought away from the wall/fence. With renvers, the hindquarters are moved towards the wall. With both movements a bend is created through the horse's body as though you were on the last step of a circle with the horse's forehead facing the direction in which he is travelling.

Travers

To help you find the correct angle and bend for this exercise, begin by riding a 10 m circle in walk at the beginning of the long side of the school. Establish a correct bend on the circle by turning your upper body, with your inside leg on the girth, so the horse has a support around which to bend. Your outside leg is behind the girth controlling the haunches; your thigh and knee prevent him losing the bend through his body and your lower leg asks his outside hind leg to step across the inside hind leg, under his body. Sit on your inside seat bone, stretch down through your inside leg to encourage the horse to move in the direction of the bend and maintain the angle of the horse's shoulders with yours. Keep your balance and position to prevent the horse going 'downhill'. Your tummy muscles will keep you supported in a tall position, with your upper body turning with the horse's body. Allowing your lower back to move with the horse's back muscles as he walks prevents you from blocking the movement by becoming too stiff. Your inside rein maintains an elastic contact with the bit to keep the horse soft and relaxed in his jaw, and your outside rein controls the outside shoulder. You may need to keep a firmer inside rein initially to keep the bend, softening the outside rein to encourage the horse to move along the track. Once he has the idea, you will be able to soften the contact on your inside rein again. This will help his inside hind leg take a bigger step, and his outside hind leg to step across under his belly.

Observe when you are approaching the last step of the circle, before the horse straightens up, this is the correct position for travers. Viewed from the front, four separate tracks will be seen, with the horse's outside legs crossing in front of his inside legs. Travers on three tracks is more advanced and requires more bend through the horse's body.

PARALLEL-POLE WORK
Set the poles out in parallel lines about 1.5 m (5 ft) apart. Put them so that you have room to ride a small circle at either end of them.

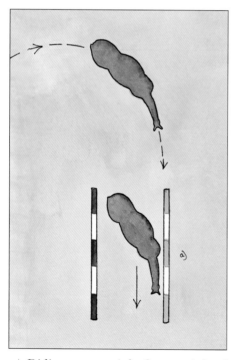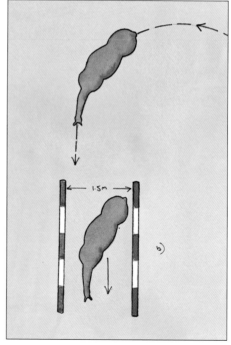

a) *Riding travers right from a right circle; b) Riding travers left from a left circle.*

TRAVERS LEFT

Ride a 10 m circle on the left rein at the end of the poles, lining yourself up to ride a travers between them. As you approach the last step of the left circle, keep the horse in this position with a half-halt. His forehand should be approaching the poles on your right with his head looking straight along them. Your right leg behind the girth asks the horse to keep his haunches to the left. Your inside leg by the girth acts as a support around which he bends, and asks him to keep stepping along forwards and sideways between the poles. He remains bent to the left through his whole body by you staying sitting on your left seat bone. Both the reins and your upper body hold the horse's forehand in position.

Approaching the poles in a travers left position clearly showing four tracks as the outside legs cross over in front of the inside legs.

Renvers

Imagine riding a 10 m circle through the fence or wall of the school. As you approach the last step of this circle (as though you have just emerged through the fence back to the track), this is the correct position for renvers. The horse's hind legs will be nearer the fence or wall than his forehand, with his forehead facing along the track in the direction of travel. The aids and angle are the same as for travers, just a mirror image.

RIDING RENVERS FROM SHOULDER-IN

Another way to introduce renvers is to develop it from shoulder-in. Changing from shoulder-in to renvers needs an obedient, supple horse, and a rider with good co-ordination of the aids. On the left rein, ride shoulder-in to the left between two parallel poles about 1.5 m (5 ft) apart. Without changing the angle of your shoulders or your hips, change your weight onto

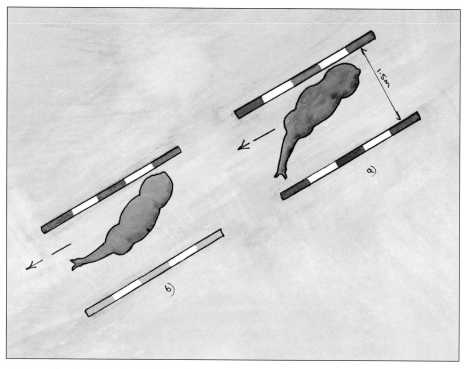

a) Start in shoulder-in left (on three tracks) between the red and blue poles.
b) Slightly increase the horse's body angle away from the green pole, and change the bend to turn the movement into renvers right (on four tracks).

your right seat bone, bring your right leg forward onto the girth, and take your left leg back behind the girth. Avoid leaning to the outside or tipping forward and keep your weight on your inside seat bone. Keep a correct bend at the front end by using both reins. Change the flexion of the horse to the right so his forehead is on the line of travel, and turn your head so you are looking between his ears. Your new inside rein (right) and new outside rein (left) will support the new bend to the right. You are now in renvers. Use frequent half-halts to maintain the balance of your horse and the rhythm of the gait. Once you have established travers and renvers in walk, in both directions, try them in a collected trot. Travers can be ridden in canter, but avoid doing too much on novice horses, as they tend to swing their haunches in anyway in canter as an evasion, so you do not want to compound the problem!

Half-pass

The half-pass encourages suppleness through the horse's body. A gymnastic horse will be able to cross his legs well and flow forwards and sideways with apparent ease. This requires powerful haunches, a strong back, and supple joints. An inexperienced horse will be less able to cross his legs as he travels forwards and sideways, so it is important to gauge the angle correctly to keep an even rhythm, and not to spoil the cadence of the gait. In lateral work, maintaining the quality of the basic gait must always take precedence over the lateral movement.

When you begin, keeping the half-pass going along a diagonal line can seem daunting, so using poles as guidelines can be useful. They help to keep your horse moving forward and sideways with his shoulders one step ahead of his hips.

Half-pass Left

Begin in walk. To ask for half-pass to the left, sit as for a left travers on four tracks. Keep your right leg behind the girth to encourage your horse to move laterally, as in travers, with your left leg on the girth asking him to step forward. The horse's outside legs cross in front of his inside legs. Concentrate on co-ordinating your leg aids to show your horse that he should move forwards and sideways at the same time. Sit up tall in the saddle, and allow your hips and lower back to follow the half-pass movement that you should feel through your horse's back as he crosses his legs. Look in the direction of travel between your horse's ears, with your chin level and with your horse's shoulders in line with your own. Both reins should keep the bend through your horse's neck correct, with the outside rein supporting the bend and the inside rein asking for flexion while remaining soft. With your inside leg on the girth, keep your horse stepping into the outside rein. As for a left circle, keep your weight to the left all the time. Reverse these aids for half-pass to the right.

V-shaped Pole Formation

Set the poles into a V shape along the diagonals of your school. No specific measurements are required, so experiment with the angle of the

V according to the angle of half-pass you wish to attempt, remembering that a steep V is harder than a shallow one. There is no point whatsoever in attempting a steep angle before a shallow one can be ridden correctly.

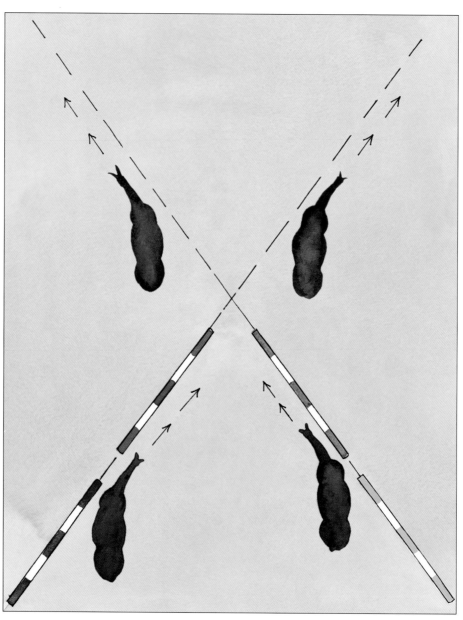

Poles set in a V shape to give a diagonal line in each direction. Begin by riding travers along the line of poles. By opening the travers so that it is on four tracks, half-pass will develop.

Begin by by riding a straight line in walk along the pole. Make sure both you and he are straight. Next, ride a four-track travers along the poles, bending in the direction your half-pass will take. The horse's forehead should be on the line of travel and you should be able to keep this position beyond the poles. If you try to keep the same angle going along the rest of the diagonal, you should have a perfect half-pass every time!

The preparation is most important. Use your upper body to position the horse well in advance. The rein contact should remain elastic if your position is correct and you have a good approach to the poles.

Half-pass developing from riding a four-track travers along the diagonal line of poles. It is important to make sure that the horse's forehand is leading in the half-pass and not his haunches.

A good attempt at a half-pass. After using the poles to set up the angle, it is easier for the rider to picture the diagonal line to ride along. The poles enable the exercise to be ridden anywhere in the arena, so the rider has the confidence to go for the line they have chosen. This horse's bend is good and he is moving well around the rider's inside leg. The horse's forehead is along the diagonal line, as is the rider's!

After you have completed as many half-pass steps as you want to, straighten the horse up again to finish the movement neatly off. This will preserve the suppleness and engagement of the hind legs that you will have achieved.

Counter Canter, Simple Changes, Flying Changes and Tempi Changes

Counter Canter

Counter canter is intentionally staying on a certain lead in canter whilst moving on the opposite rein, for example maintaining left lead whilst moving to the right. It is a test of your horse's balance, strength and obedience to your aids. You must also be well balanced and sure of what you are asking your horse to do!

To begin, set two poles in a wide V shape at one end of the school. At the other end, place a plastic cone as a marker for the centre point of a 20 m circle. Warm your horse up, establishing a good collected canter via frequent transitions into and out of canter, first from trot then from walk.

Counter canter around the school using one or two poles 1.5 m (5 ft) in from the fence to prevent the haunches from swinging to the left. The rider keeps her position for right canter, maintaining a bend to the right.

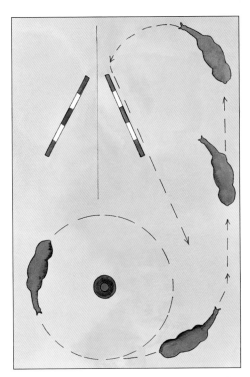

A plastic barrel marking the centre of a 20 m circle. Ride a shoulder-fore up the long side, maintaining the same bend along the pole.

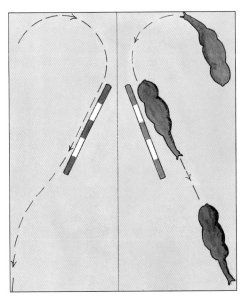

Follow the pole back to the track, maintaining the bend.

A forward-thinking collected canter is ideal for riding counter canter. Your horse must have developed some ability to keep his weight on his hocks in order for you to ride counter canter. A useful preparation exercise in walk and trot is shoulder-fore, which helps you to feel the amount of bend that your horse needs through his body. The shoulder-fore position is required for a good counter canter. Practise it in both walk and trot, using the whole school, including the corners.

Riding the whole school in shoulder-fore towards the wall (counter bend) is also helpful for your position. Always use your aids in a co-ordinated way to ensure the required bend in your horse.

Using the cone as the centre marker, ride a 20 m circle on the left rein in trot at one end of the school. When your horse feels balanced, ride up the long side to the other end, maintaining the bend to the left in shoulder-fore. Look at where the pole nearest to you is and ride a half circle left towards it so that you can follow it back to the track. At this stage, it does not matter which side of the pole you ride along so long as you choose in advance. Ultimately, as you turn more neatly, you want to be on the side of the pole nearest the wall. As you approach the wall in trot, smoothly continue along the track keeping the bend to the left through your horse. His shoulders should now be turned slightly towards the wall. Before the corner, straighten and walk. Repeat this on the other rein, setting the bend up on the circle.

Next, repeat the whole exercise in canter. You should be able to canter a circle of about 12–15 m in diameter, keeping your horse balanced and on the correct canter lead before starting the counter canter. Maintain your leg position throughout the counter-canter exercise. If you move your legs the other way around by mistake, your horse may change canter lead or become disunited. Establish the true canter on the 20 m circle and go up the long side, keeping the bend and your leg position with your inside leg on the girth and your outside leg behind. Do not move your body as you turn down the pole towards the wall in counter canter; instead, you should be positioned as though you are going to canter through the wall. Keep your weight in the inside stirrup of the canter and look between your horse's ears. If you change your head position, you risk him changing lead! The real test is riding a 20 m circle in counter canter. Try this exercise once you are able to ride half circles of about 12–15 m in counter canter easily. If you encounter problems return to walk and start again. This keeps your horse calm and prevents confusion.

Simple Changes

A simple change involves changing the canter lead through walk. Set two poles across the centre point of the school about 2 m (6½ ft) apart. At each end of the school, mark the centre of a 20 m circle with a plastic barrel. Establish a calm, collected canter with plenty of lift off the ground, otherwise your horse will not have enough time to change leg. For example, canter on a left circle round one of the cones. Approach the poles from the circle and make a transition to walk. Reposition your horse with a right bend and ask for right canter onto the other circle. In this way, ride a large figure of eight, each time passing through the poles with a simple change through walk. Make sure that you can place your horse accurately between the poles so that he is straight for a moment in between the canters. This gives you time to alter your leg position. Repeat the exercise, beginning with right canter. Although your horse will probably favour one or the other, it is important to practise the exercise from both directions.

Approaching the poles from left canter, half-halt with your body and your

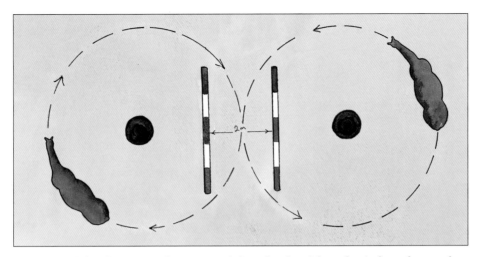

Two parallel poles across the centre of the school, with a plastic barrel at each end marking the centres of the 20 m circles.

existing outside rein (right). Even up your legs and your seat so that you are sitting straight, and walk three or four steps. Prepare for right canter with your left leg back, right leg on the girth and sit on your right seat bone. Turn your shoulders slightly right and ask for canter with your outside leg. Speaking from personal experience, if your horse does not understand that he should canter from your outside leg aid first, you will always have problems with flying changes. Your horse's outside hind leg starts the canter off, so it follows that your outside leg asks first, just a split second before your inside leg tells him to go. Reverse these aids for left canter.

Flying Changes

Once you find simple changes easy, eliminate the walk steps and change your position directly from left canter to right. A flying change involves your horse changing his canter lead from one to the other in the moment of suspension within one canter stride. The canter must have enough spring to ensure that your horse has time to change his legs in mid air!

Clear, well-timed aids are vital. Your legs need to be hanging without tension from the hips; otherwise, your horse will not be able to change lead! Smoothly change your seat and leg position, remembering to turn your upper body at the same time. Although the change in the rider's position should be definite, it should also be subtle. Throwing your upper body from side to side will just unbalance the horse. It seems like a lot to do at once, but if you just think of changing from one position to the other in one smooth movement, it should work! As your new outside leg comes back, give your horse a nudge with your calf to bring his new outside hind leg through to start the new canter. Your rein contact must stay elastic. As you approach the change, think about keeping your horse as straight as possible through his neck. Keep your reins level and soften your new inside rein as your horse changes to allow his leading leg to come through.

Keep training sessions for flying changes separate from counter canter and have different exercises for each while you are both learning. Some degree of counter canter is inevitable when training for flying changes. It would be wrong to

An accurate flying change from a collected canter, clearly springing off the ground, performed between two poles to help keep the horse straight.

unbalance the horse for the sake of a flying change when a few steps of counter canter would help the preparation. Only try a few flying changes during any one training session – it is easy to overdo it and spoil your horse's canter rhythm. It may take time to perfect the movement, and frantic efforts on your part will be counter-productive.

Tempi Changes

Straightness when riding tempi-changes is vital, otherwise riding a series of changes across the diagonal of the dressage arena becomes a wavy line with the horse swinging from side to side!

Riding between poles, ride simple changes through walk (see page 178) every fourth stride. Once you can do this easily, try one flying change to the left, for example, then one to the right on the fourth canter stride afterwards. Keep the canter rhythm regular. When you can ride simple changes every three strides, try flying changes every three strides, then every two strides, and finally every stride. Keep your upper body and your horse's forehand straight, maintaining a steady contact with the bit, and just change your hip and leg position for each successive change in a smooth motion to avoid excessive movement from your body, which would disturb the fluency of the changes. Soften your fingers on your new inside rein with each change to allow the new inside leg to step forwards.

Piaffe

Piaffe is a trot-like movement executed on the spot. The horse is allowed to travel forward slightly at each step, but not at the expense of placing the feet in diagonal pairs. Most of the horse's weight is taken on the hind legs, allowing the forehand to lift. Each foreleg lifts to a near-horizontal position with the front hooves as high as midcannon bone. Each hind leg lifts to the point where the hind hooves are level with the pasterns. They cannot lift much higher than this if the hindquarters are carrying most of the weight of the horse.

Piaffe develops from your horse being strong enough in his back and hind limbs to take a greater proportion of his weight on his haunches than on his forehand. In a correct piaffe, your horse should give the impression of lowering his haunches and bending his hocks, tucking his pelvis under him. His forehand should appear to lift with his neck well arched and his poll the highest point. This is only achieved with a correctly trained and well-balanced horse. However, most horses will piaffe beautifully without a rider when they are excited – usually when cavorting around in the field. The trick is to reproduce this when we are in the saddle!

Preparation Work

To begin these exercises, set the poles out in a V formation in the middle of your school. You will enter the V through the wide part and exit through the narrow end.

Lay out four poles close enough to ride a collected walk over them, i.e. about 0.8 m (2½ ft), or a small human step, at a distance of 7 m (23 ft) before the V.

Prepare your horse with some lateral work in walk and trot, mixing and matching the movements so that your horse is really listening to your aids. Switch from shoulder-in to travers and from shoulder-out to renvers, then do exercises which involve changing the bend, such as shoulder-in to shoulder-

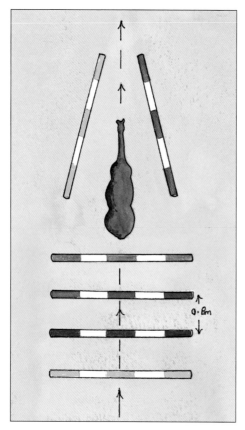

Parallel poles set at 0.8 m (2½ ft) apart for a collected walk, followed by a V through which to ride piaffe steps.

out and travers to renvers. Frequent transitions will also help your horse to engage his hocks. Strategic transitions can divide lateral exercise into manageable chunks, so that you and your horse do not end up twiddling around all over the place. Do not forget to go large now and again in medium or extended gaits to increase the energy and revitalize your collected work. Collected work is very demanding on a horse's musculature, so the more extended work is also physically necessary.

Rein-back is a good preparation for piaffe because it increases the weight-carrying potential of your horse's haunches and helps him to understand how to move forward with a great deal of collection.

When you are ready, walk towards the parallel poles. Ride over them keeping your horse collected throughout and then extend the stride towards the V and ride straight through it to keep your horse thinking forward as he passes through the V. Approach again and walk over the poles as before. This time, start asking for more collection immediately after the poles so that you are almost walking on the spot, but be sure to maintain a forward impulse to prevent your horse from thinking that you want to go backwards.

To ask for a very collected walk, sit up as tall as you can in the saddle. Ease your thighs back and down, with both of your feet slightly behind the girth, as you would for rein-back. Continue sitting up straight, which is essential to help your horse remain in balance. Keep your ribcage lifted up and ease your weight towards the front of your seat. Do not overdo this otherwise you will end up perching too far forward with a very hollow back. Maintain the walk motion through your lower back so you do not become stiff. Keep stretching up through your stomach and visualize lifting your horse off the ground with your stomach, thighs and knees, without gripping. Keep your thighs long and back underneath you. You do not need legs like iron bars, but they must stay in position, holding and lifting your horse as though your legs are attached with Velcro to his sides.

Maintain an elastic contact as your horse lifts through his neck and poll, keeping your hands soft as you hold the reins with your elbows still and your shoulders relaxed. Look ahead; if you look down or poke your chin out you will negatively affect your horse's balance.

Maintain this light, upright seat after walking through the poles. Then, keeping your legs in the same position, ask with both lower legs together, as you would ask for trot. If you have a nice long schooling whip, or a piaffe whip, give your horse a few encouraging taps behind – ideally on your horse's thigh, if you can reach this far back.

Progressing to Piaffe-like Steps

Imagine trotting on the spot in a two-time rhythm. As soon as your horse begins piaffe steps, let your legs hang more quietly by his sides. You will then be able to use them alternately to keep the rhythm, but keep your aids subtle otherwise you risk disturbing the regularity of the steps. If your hips are free enough, your legs will almost do this by remote control, as your horse's slight movement will do it for you. Avoid swinging your seat from side to side, as this will cause your horse to rock when he should remain straight and steady. Try this for a few steps, then walk.

Allow these piaffe-like steps to advance towards the V of poles. Your horse should remain in the same outline, holding his balance and self-carriage. This proves to you that he is working correctly. You should feel that you could control the steps with your seat, rather than holding him up in front with the reins.

As the poles of the V become closer together, collect the piaffe-like steps until your horse is almost working on the spot. Half steps forwards are good enough for the first few months of this advanced training. Your horse can only progress gradually to a full-blown piaffe, moving very slightly forward as he does it, after many months of training, because he has to build up enough muscular strength to carry himself in this extreme collection. Do not ask too much too often, and follow up by riding forward in medium or extended trot strides to refresh the gait and utilize the impulsion you will have created.

Set three or four cavalletti at about 0.8 m (2½ ft) apart and two poles alongside each other about 1.5 m (5 ft) apart after them. Ride collected walk over the cavalletti and progress to piaffe-like steps between the

Progressing to piaffe-like steps using a pole to help keep the horse straight.

poles to help keep your horse straight.

If you are doing the exercise correctly, all of the movement should be going on through his leg joints which act like shock absorbers. You should feel a slight pulsation through his back muscles as he picks his feet up. Immediately pick up the rhythm in your own body and remember that your horse cannot piaffe unless you do, too. Imagine softly absorbing his movement through your lumbar back. As soon as you feel him take piaffe-like steps, soften the reins without giving them totally away.

Remember that, barring problems, it takes about four years to train a horse to advanced level from scratch. It is useful for both you and your horse to enjoy playing with the more advanced movements, provided that you are aware that the essentials must be correct, such as his outline, balance, confidence and, most important, your position and aids!

An advanced-level horse showing the engagement of the hocks needed for piaffe. The forearms should lift to a near-horizontal position with the front hooves as high as the midcannon bones. The hind legs lift to the point where the hind hooves are level with the pasterns.

Passage

Passage is a floating, forward movement executed in the phase of the trot with a clearly defined period of suspension. The horse has to push off the ground from his diagonal pairs of legs, unlike piaffe, where the hind legs carry the weight. It requires a horse to have the muscular development and balance that will enable him to spring off the ground at each step, travelling forward as he does so. A correct passage springs rhythmically off the ground, with the horse maintaining his outline with his haunches tucked under him and good articulation of his leg joints. His legs should come off the ground in diagonal pairs with the hind feet lifting as high as his pasterns, and his front feet as high as his midcannon bones (the same as in piaffe) and the two-beat trot rhythm must remain regular.

Some horses prefer passage to piaffe, but the drawback is that they tend to go into passage to evade performing piaffe. This may be for purely physical reasons – some horses, because of their conformation, find piaffe extremely difficult. Unfortunately, it is relatively easy to pop into a 'false' passage from a collected trot. If you are not able to keep your horse's outline absolutely correct, the danger is that he will spring forward in an effort to leave his back legs out behind. By doing this he will fall onto his forehand and become hollow and above the bit.

Preparation Work

To begin these exercises, set out parallel poles close enough to ride a collected trot over them: they should be about 0.8–1 m (3 ft) apart.

Warm your horse up with lateral work to supple him up and ride variations within each gait, especially in the trot work. Work your way around the school changing from collected trot to working, medium and extended trot as your horse becomes more supple and energized. Energy is the key factor here, because your horse must be thinking forward and be light to your aids. If he needs some improvement in this area, make frequent transitions with just a few strides in between to sharpen him up and make him more alert. Remember to do halt transitions and ensure that they are square and well balanced. The aim of this is to make sure that your horse can keep his self-carriage while working with a great deal of impulsion.

To ask for passage, you need to be in a tall, upright position, allowing the

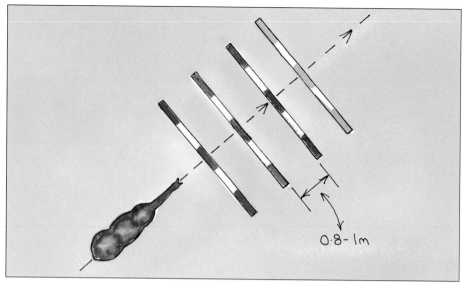

Parallel poles set at about 0.8–1m (3 ft) apart for a collected trot.

horse's back to lift underneath you, with your thighs back and down and your feet just behind the girth, in the same way as they are for piaffe. You must remain vertical while making the adjustments in your seat. Your weight has to allow your horse to move forward with great energy, even though his progression in mph is slow, in order for him to spring off the ground. Your hips should be fractionally pressed forward, but do not

Horse and rider growing more upright to help develop the springy, elevated steps needed for passage.

overdo it or you will end up in piaffe. Avoid hollowing your back too much and sticking your backside out.

From a collected trot, increase the strength and muscle tone of your position. Increase the suspension of the trot with your thighs and knees, imagining that you are both springing up and down. Keep your stomach muscles strong to support your back and to lift you both off the ground. Ask for trot with your lower legs in a steady rhythm as you strengthen your position. Maintain an upright position and have the feeling that you are lifting your horse off the ground. As soon as you feel him start to spring, allow your legs to hang by his sides. Press him forward with your lower-leg aids to keep the momentum in a forward direction. You should feel dramatic, lofty steps!

Your lumbar back must act as a shock absorber, which is aided by your stomach muscles. Avoid becoming floppy around the middle or you will lose the passage and your horse will take off – it is a bit like taking the handbrake off too quickly! You need to be both strong and supple in your own body to ride a good passage.

If your horse is genuinely in need of encouragement, carry your schooling whip behind you so that you can tap him on top of his croup. Regular, rhythmic taps will give him the idea of bouncing in the passage. This only works in conjunction with correct leg and seat aids; using the whip is emphatically not a substitute for the aids. Horses who have been trained just with the whip and incorrect aids tend to bounce their bottoms up and down with the front feet shuffling on the spot. This false passage appears heavy and looks as though the horse is stuck on the ground.

Maintain the outline of your horse's neck with elastic reins, developing a feel through your whole arm so that you can make fine adjustments to the contact through your fingers while keeping your arm position constant. All horses appreciate having a steady bridle to work into which helps them to correct their balance and self-carriage by altering their posture rather than backing away from the bit and becoming tense. Avoid fiddling with the contact, as you will not feel the subtleties required. Now you need to fine-tune everything for ultimate softness and roundness.

Progressing to Passage

Just ride a few steps of passage at a time then refresh your horse by going off in medium or extended trot, depending on the amount of elevation you have achieved in the passage. The test of a good passage is if you can then

The elevated steps of passage with the hind feet lifting as high as his pasterns, and his front feet as high as the midcannon bones (the same as in piaffe).

ride forward in improved self-carriage with increased energy. Passage should be like coiling up a spring ready for release, not plodding and heavy. Return to the collected trot over the poles at intervals to remind your horse to take even steps with all four legs and re-establish the rhythm if he has lost it. This session should last about fifteen minutes. If you have problems, rather than continuing for too long, return to simple trotting poles and keep the steps going around the school. Frequent stretching and thinking time for you both is important to prevent tension creeping in.

Passage can be developed from riding the piaffe but in the early stages you may prefer to keep training sessions for passage separate from piaffe. As you ask for piaffe from collected walk, have a different approach to establish passage and ask for it from a collected trot. This will prevent either you or your horse from becoming confused. Train these movements in separate sessions for the same reason.

While it may be useful to teach the movements separately, the advanced tests contain transitions between piaffe and passage. These are extremely difficult transitions and should only be attempted once you and your horse are confident with the separate exercises and you feel that you are both at the required standard. Your horse may think otherwise, though, and might surprise you with passage or piaffe when you least expect it! If this happens, do not tell him off, but pretend you wanted it anyway, resuming your original exercise at an opportune moment. It is important to refresh the trot by riding forward at regular intervals during and after collected work. Transitions such as passage to extended trot, and extended trot to passage will develop when your horse is strong in his back, supple and well balanced.

Index